MUSLIMS
—— IN ——
EUROPE

MUSLIMS
—— IN ——
EUROPE

NOTES, COMMENTS, QUESTIONS

MANFRED WOLF

MUSLIMS IN EUROPE
NOTES, COMMENTS, QUESTIONS

iUniverse books may be ordered through booksellers or by contacting:

iUniverse
1663 Liberty Drive
Bloomington, IN 47403
www.iuniverse.com
1-800-Authors (1-800-288-4677)

ISBN: 978-1-5320-3019-2 (sc)
ISBN: 978-1-5320-3020-8 (e)

Print information available on the last page.

iUniverse rev. date: 08/24/2017

Praise for *Almost a Foreign Country*:

"... offers the interesting perspective of an immigrant who has absorbed a large part of American culture but questions the rest ..."
— Kirkus Discoveries

"... Here is another fable of America, as seen by another wise foreign-born writer (Nabokov comes to mind) whose love for his adopted country is coupled with keen-witted irony and a total absence of sentimental cant ..."
— Maurice Bassan, Amazon.com

Praise for *Survival in Paradise*:

"... Wolf's page-turning, thrill-a-minute first chapter, "1942", reads like an outline for a big-screen Hollywood thriller."
— Glenn Gullmes, *West Portal Monthly*

"... Although the ostensible purpose of the author is to describe his own coming to terms with his family's horrific near-unsuccessful escape from a hellish end, he ... chronicle[s] a history of the entire range of varied reactions by many of the cohort of fleeing Jews ..."
— Vernon Miles Kerr, *Westside Observer*

Acknowledgments

Most of the essays written before 2008 have appeared earlier, some in slightly different form, in my book *Almost a Foreign Country*, published in 2008. Many of them had been published earlier in various American newspapers.

The essay called "Young Moroccans in the Netherlands: Crime and Radicalism" is a revision of a much longer conference paper read for me at the American Association of Netherlandic Studies Conference, Chapel Hill, North Carolina, June 7, 2008, and published in *Dutch Studies in a Globalized World*, ed. Margriet Bruijn Lacy (2009).

My long-distance friendship with the Dutch-Moroccan scholar Youssef Azghari got its start when I wrote about his first book, *Cultuurbepaalde Communicatie*, for the San Francisco Chronicle. Since then, he and I have co-authored two essays, "Identity and Diversity: Muslims in the US and Europe," first published in *The West Portal Monthly* and in a Dutch version in *NRC Handelsblad*, December 1, 2007, and reprinted in other publications, principally the *International Psychology Bulletin*. The second co-written piece, "Acculturating Muslims in the West: More Complex in Europe than America," also first appeared in *The West*

Portal Monthly and then in Dutch in a collection of articles called *Waarom haten ze ons eigenlijk?* (2016). I am happy to be able to include all three pieces here.

The essays written after 2008 were first published in *The West Portal Monthly*, except for "Of Masks and Burkas," which came out in *The Sacramento Bee* on February 24, 2017.

I have been pleased to learn a good deal from a number of friends, principally my Brandeis University classmate, the anthropologist Herbert Lewis; the writer and teacher Christopher Thornton of Zayed University, in Dubai, who has written extensively about the Middle East; and the Dutch classicist and cultural historian, the late J.P. Guépin, whose books, especially *Weg met de boheme* (1992) and *Het humanisme* (1993), strengthened my conviction that the modern bourgeoisie could be a liberalizing force and, surprisingly, a protector of humanistic impulses. I have written about Guépin at some length in "Fanatic Moderation: The Unconventional Wisdom of J.P. Guépin," *Vantage Points. Publications of the American Assn. of Netherlandic Studies #10* (1996), and I continue to wish that his brilliant work were available in English.

I am grateful to all my correspondents who have taken the time to write me, sometimes angrily, about my columns as they appeared. A few are mentioned by name in the pieces themselves.

I am also grateful to Glenn Gullmes, the editor of *The West Portal Monthly*, for his support of my column, This Time, This Place.

And finally I wish to underscore my deep gratitude to Yael Abel, whose practical help, computer-savvy, and imaginative editorial advice helped make this book possible.

MW

Contents

Acknowledgments... vii
Introduction.. xiii

Culture and Style

Generalizations about Them and Us.........................3
Personal Style and Cultural Mode.........................6
Two Ways of Looking at the World.........................9
In Praise of Facts......................................12
Amnesty and the Enduring Question of Immigration....14
Culture Change—and Culture Clash.......................17
On Masks and Burkas....................................20

World In Turmoil

Christmas Thoughts on Peace and War....................25
Bleak Thoughts on the First Decade: Reflections and
    Predictions..28
A Very Long-Range Prediction...........................31

Terrorism

Stalkers and Terrorists: The Emotional Connection........37

Human Behavior and Foreign Policy: A Parallel 40
September 11, 2001 43
The "Message" They Send Is Really About Us 46
In the Wake of the Paris Attacks 49
What Goes Into Radicalization?—An Imaginary
    Profile 52
The Rabbi and the Terrorist 55

Recent Past: Accommodation and Extremism

Death of Pim Fortuyn: End of the Great Dutch Social
    Experiment? 61
European Anger: Fighting the Wrong Battle 64
Europe Emboldens Its Muslim Women 67
Complexities of Integrating Muslims into Europe 72
Muslims in Europe: Yet Another Dilemma—Or a
    Passing Phase? 76

Present Decade: Moderation and Stridency

What About the Moderate Muslims? 81
Barriers Against Assimilating Europe's Muslims 84
The Silent Majority, the Strident Minority 87
"Muslims in Europe": Answer to Some of my Critics ... 90
Well-Meaning Misconceptions about Muslims in
    Europe 93

Affinity and Acculturation

Do Arabs Communicate Differently? 99
Theft and Survival 102
Identity and Diversity: Muslims in the US and
    Europe (with Youssef Azghari) 107

Young Moroccans in the Netherlands: Crime and
    Radicalism.. 111
Acculturating Muslims in the West: More Complex
    in Europe than America (with Youssef Azghari).....118
Elusive Affinities: New Cultures in Europe...................123
Two Cultures, Two Attitudes 126

Afterword: Muslims in Europe: Notes, Comments,
    Questions..129

Introduction

I first started writing essays on the subject of Muslims in Europe in the 1970s and 1980s after several visits to the Netherlands. The physical appearance of the country I remembered so keenly from early childhood had changed, of course, as had what Holland had looked like in more recent times. In the big cities, groups of men in Arab dress stood around, often staring gloomily, even to my eyes angrily, at their surroundings, while their women, fully covered up, were busily shopping, buying groceries, yelling in Arabic or Turkish after their children.

The grim silence of the men, the contrast between the women and the often revealingly dressed native Dutch girls and women, were a visible reminder of a new and important presence.

A few years later, in Belgium and especially France, I had a sense of larger exotic crowds but somehow less of a contrasting presence. Could France's long association with Algeria and Morocco have made for a feeling of greater affinity between French and Arab?

On subsequent trips to Europe, in the 1980s and 90s, I became aware of Moroccans having become an officially designated "problem" in the Netherlands, rowdiness and crime being linked to their presence. I went to a panel discussion in an Amsterdam night club (yes!), where one panelist assured the audience that Moroccan gays wanted what Dutch gays did, but another panelist chided Moroccans for having "no sense of irony" and "lacking in any capacity for self-criticism." The latter was applauded raucously as well as jeered.

Widely read books started appearing, first by Frits Bolkestein, then later on by Pim Fortuyn, warning against the "Islamizing" of the Netherlands. Many similarly oriented books came out in other European countries, e.g., by the Frenchman Alain Finkielkraut, or the Italian Oriana Fallaci.

A few years later, I had yet another feeling. The more recent arrivals were often not the children and grandchildren of guest workers but refugees, as I had been as a child and adolescent. Were these people not another version of all the people I had known during my adolescence in Curacao? And were they not deserving of the same attention so many had lavished on me? Why should I of all people see them as a problem?

Meanwhile, the Europeans had started complaining, about North African young toughs, about their forming separate "islands," their unwillingness to "integrate." The battle had been joined.

All these feelings and questions were the original impulse for my interest in the subject. But I also became fascinated with the way my subject changed as I started tracing it and became immersed in it.

In later essays I analyzed some of the problems I've observed, their different aspects, their implications for Europe and for us. While my original intention had been to develop them into a coherent book, I finally felt that by reprinting them more or less as I had written them, I could give my reader a sense of how the subject evolved in my own thinking. They form a kind of background to what's happening, and are meant to be suggestive, exploratory, quizzical, and somewhat open-ended.

As these pieces were published, I remember being looked at askance. Why was I turning this subject into a problem? Wasn't immigration always difficult? Especially Americans but also many Europeans said, "It may be a bit of a problem now, but in a few generations it won't. Look at postwar Portuguese immigrants to the Netherlands, or the nineteenth century Irish and Italians in America. After a while, newcomers assimilate. That's just how it is."

I sensed that far more was involved here, but in the early days I felt most strongly that the fault lay with both sides. The Europeans were reluctant to let their Arab arrivals into "the family," while the newcomers did not assimilate well and were sometimes reluctant to do so. That remains my conviction. But I also started seeing the problem as a multi-faceted incompatibility of cultures, where one culture would ultimately have to submit to the other. My view of integration was, and is, that true multiculturalism within one society has a hard time existing, and that inevitably the norms and values of one culture have to prevail, in subtle and unsubtle ways.

When that did not happen, all sorts of opinions were floated by those in government and the academy whose job it is to explain it. Arabs were not accepted, or were angry about past colonialism, or rebelled against societies that preached tolerance but were not tolerant, or they were fighting poverty, or were angry because their own culture was denigrated, etc. These were all convenient explanations, but, in my view, palpably untrue. It has become part of the posturing of our time to allege grave injustices, not because there aren't any, but because it's so much easier and more politically acceptable to take the supposed victim's word for it than to look at the complicated reality with its manifold complexities.

Both high crime figures, and later even terrorism, were explained this way, when in my mind the explanation lay with a fairly specific form of cultural stress, one culture chafing at the ways of the other to which it had in some way to bend, or at the very least could not be persuaded or seduced to give its heart to. Inevitably this did not afflict the majority of immigrants but a significant minority. Those who took to the new culture, whether in Belgium, the Netherlands, or Germany, tended to thrive emotionally and economically. They became "acculturated." Like the Irish in America, or the Italians, they did not turn into separate countries—they "dissolved" —and one question this book asks is whether the others will "dissolve" too.

The resistance to seeing the problem this way is to this day intense. It sounds condescending. It goes against a certain sophisticated relativism. It smacks of the right-wing or a form of Samuel Huntington's Clash of Civilizations. But to my mind it is not any of these things. Simply stated, some cultures, like some married couples, do not get along under the same roof. We all know the outcome of that.

In my essays I try to outline what these incompatibilities are and, less precisely, what they may portend. A kind of Islam-induced absolutism clings to the cultures of the Middle East and North Africa. A literalism of religion and a stern adherence to cultural precept affects many of those who, generations later, struggle with what they see as the moral vacuum of the West. A pleasurably secret love for the old ways affects even those who never knew what the old ways were, and now hear them explained by glib imams on the Internet. A sense of their new home as being economically prosperous but morally and psychologically impoverished is the dry tinder that can be set alight by politics, self-righteousness, or even long-smoldering resentment.

Add to this that Western European cultures do not come on as strong as American cultures do. The "soft" power of America lies in its ubiquitous, seductive insistence on its movies, its music, its slang, while European cultures tend to be more self-effacing— especially following the drive for a peaceful united Europe after World War Two. Dutch culture, for example, is quietly unassertive, while America is unabashedly loud. Moreover, Western cultures stress certain freedoms and rights as their values, but these can look pale and anemic or appear as merely political beliefs and, worse, a sign of ethical and moral bankruptcy.

If I have made any contribution to this subject, it is to point to these cultural differences as far more important than any other.

San Francisco, 2017

Culture and Style

Generalizations about Them and Us

In the early years of the twentieth century, people might sit in a Parisian sidewalk cafe and happily try to guess from which country the strolling passersby came. Those were the days when it was fine to talk about "national character" and to stereotype people according to the way in which their culture was perceived.

Now, of course, this is not a way we talk about other cultures. It's politically incorrect to do so, and we don't believe in such large-scale characterizations of whole nations and groups.

Or do we? After all, we use the terms "cultural traits" quite as openly as people once did "national character," and we have no hesitation in discussing "cultural patterns," or saying, "That's the way they do it in their culture." So maybe the following remarks about Them and Us are less reckless and retrograde than they appear.

1) The Arab Middle Eastern world loves intrigue, often for its own sake: the goal seems secondary. The various parties in this intrigue shift all the time, because finally it doesn't matter who your allies are, as long as you can

keep 'intriguing'. All that slyness and plotting leads...
where exactly?

Syria, we are told, is working together with Iran in order
to bolster the Iraqi insurgency. Sunni Iraqis collaborate
with the Syrians in order to undermine the Shiites. But
the Shiites in Iraq work with the Shiites in Iran against the
Americans—and the Sunnis. Have we come full circle yet?

One reason conspiracy theories are so popular in the
Arab world is that there are so many conspiracies. And one
reason why these conspiracy theories often seem to change
is that the conspiracies themselves may well shift often in
the shifting sands of the Middle East.

2) The U.S. proclivity, on the other hand, is a lust for
planning multiple contingencies and producing exciting
scenarios. We are never so happy as when we can turn
the world into high-tech video games: "They do this,
and we do that. . . . Look at the screen. . . . Zap!"
Handshakes all around the "Situation Room" or, gasp,
the "War Room." Understated, manly compliments.
"Nice work, General!" Or sometimes even, "Heck of
a job!"

The ultimate aim is security or victory, sure, but the
pleasure is in the many forms of 'gaming' and warfare. We
live in a culture of preadolescent boys lasting into manhood
and even dotage.

Long before 9/11, we were obsessed with thrillers, spy
movies, gadgets, espionage, and game playing. That horrible
day—often compared to a ghastly film—merely crystallized
what had already obtained, the proliferation of images we
watch and attempt to defend against and manipulate.

The Cold War before then had supplied an abundance of pictures. Not that there weren't plenty of real enemies—of course there were. But we loved the struggle, we enjoyed the plans and counterplans. Careers were made, money flowed, but best of all was the gaming, the multiple reports, always filed, almost always forgotten. Rather than read an old report, start the fun all over again and write a new one.

Meanwhile, you could be important enough to turn your life into a kind of movie. And you could create names and acronyms, and these would be respectfully repeated. Remember "Mutually Assured Destruction," "MAD"?

The lines between warfare and its media portrayals blurred. You could be a warrior by going into a room and fiddling with buttons and looking at a screen. Afterwards, your colleagues might literally applaud your playing. What could be better?

These two cultural styles do not, of course, sum up their respective cultures. But they do reveal something our leaders do not often see, and they lay bare a significant side of the present-day clash between the two.

2005

Personal Style and Cultural Mode

Every once in a while I come across someone whose manner of winning friends or relating to people astonishes me because it's so different from most people's. He or she tends to want to bribe, bully, browbeat, or badger someone into friendship. If the other person is seen as important, then a certain flattery may be involved too; somehow status gets into the whole equation.

I suppose we all do some of it. A measure of seduction is part of the early overtures. You ingratiate yourself with the other by being attentive or kind or doing small favors, but most people would certainly not pursue or harass another. And they would inevitably see that approach as counterproductive.

It sounds a bit as if I'm writing about stalking here, or some sort of Cable Guy syndrome, but while it comes close to those, it's not quite what I have in mind.

I refer to an initial pattern of pursuit. The sought-after friend becomes the object of many telephone calls; there is no waiting for him or her to respond, no sense of the other person needing to develop a set of corresponding feelings. Somehow affection or its natural growth aren't understood;

a kind of aggressive wooing takes the shape of a play for power. The other person must be forced to respond, and you seize his friendship, you conquer it.

The people who do this do not understand how most ordinary, normal relationships develop. They see waiting for the other person to call as a sign of weakness. If they telephone five times a day, they feel they're expressing interest, not badgering. They reach out in the only way they can.

In fact, by calling it badgering or bullying, I am merely expressing my bias and that of the society in which I live.

They are, of course, sadly out of step with how these things are generally done in our culture. I have long felt that one source of human unhappiness is for a person to be ill-suited to the culture he grows up in, or the parents he has, or the social setting into which he was born.

But are there really cultures where this behavior is acceptable rather than pathological?

I know I'm on anthropologically slippery ground here, but I suspect that some cultures encourage, promote or incarnate this way of doing things. Such a style might have been infinitely more acceptable in nineteenth century Russia, or may be much more the norm in present-day Saudi Arabia.

In large parts of the world, it's expected that you approach the other through flattery, bribery, and, if need be, marks of your own subservience. If you are responded to, a bond ensues. If you are rebuffed or ignored, a passionate anger results. That anger is widely understood as a legitimate response to rejection, and not scorned. It might well set in motion a whole series of feuds. Such is the dominant cultural style.

The interplay of personal style and dominant cultural mode may well be the most important ingredient in the successful integration of immigrant groups into a new culture. Those who have always been out of step with their own culture find themselves thriving if their personal patterns match the new culture's. You can imagine an even-tempered Arab immigrant doing better in Europe, assimilating more successfully, than his fiercer, more tumultuous counterpart.

Other experiences remain important, of course, but I submit that the compatibility of personality traits with dominant cultural styles is crucial.

2009

Two Ways of Looking at the World

I read the following brief piece in the June '09 issue of "De Krant," a monthly newspaper for people of Dutch origin living in Canada and the United States. Here's my translation:

"The Amsterdam police has been dealing with a devout Muslim who scratches off advertising posters from billboards with his fingernails.

"On these billboards, sexy ladies advertise the lingerie brand Sapph. The man, Tarix Abdullah, says he acts 'out of respect for God.' He says he doesn't have anything against women, but does when they wear nothing more than bra and panties. 'I do this to protect women and children who pass by here. Women shouldn't think they have to look like this in order to please men. If they follow God's path, especially that of Islam, we can avert the danger,' he let it be known."

That says it all, doesn't it? This little news clipping is a perfect poem, a haiku, of two ways of looking at the world, two styles of thinking.

The man does what he does "to protect women." The infringement on their freedom is for their benefit, to save them, to protect them from lustful, prying eyes, from the desire to ravish them.

This is how we show our respect, says the Muslim. How can the West not see this? It's not an infringement on their freedom but a way of shielding them from harm. To keep evil at bay is not a denial of freedom.

The West, of course, defines its respect for women by affirming their freedom to do what they want, by leaving them alone, by not interfering with them, by allowing them to display themselves.

Each side acts out of a certain sincerity, or at any rate sees itself as acting sincerely. Never mind that there is an undercurrent of sadistic pleasure in shaming women by restricting them and covering them up—never mind too that there is an element of (largely male) exploitation in these Western women showing off their bodies. In the debates, both sides look away from what undermines their own position—or don't see what does.

In fact, there is yet another aspect to this matter of freedom. If girls in the West are free, and free to display themselves, this freedom quickly spills over into excess. You can take off your clothes, but you should also be free to make a pornographic movie. If you can divorce, you should be free to divorce ten times. The point is that nobody knows where ordinary freedom spills over into excess— excess itself is a subjective concept. Your ten divorces strike me as excessive, but why should they? Who am I to say?

And the Muslim desire to "protect" women, where does it stop? The head scarf is clearly not enough—how about a burka? And best not to let those desirable, licentious creatures leave the house. Their only function should be to serve the men in the family. Ultimately, the desire to protect comes down to a male war against women. Just ask any woman who lives under the Taliban.

But Tarix has yet another concern. He seeks to keep women from falling into error. He means to save them from thinking dangerously. They should know they don't have to be in their underwear to attract men. They don't have to be victimized by sexual stereotyping. Odd that here Western feminism meets extremist Islam. Both agree that women shouldn't think that physical beauty and displaying feminine attributes are the path to attracting men. That can—or should—be done in other ways. Tarix thinks that Islam can offer that ultimate path.

Despite this particular intersection, the two ways of thinking are so divergent that they cannot be reconciled. Muslim and Western—fundamentalist and liberal—religious and progressive—they are not simply going to adapt to each other. Tarix's work with billboards is just beginning.

2009

In Praise of Facts

"He's always late," we say when a friend keeps us waiting, even though more than half the time he's punctual. We get exasperated, we exaggerate, and don't care about being factual. Emotions, of course, fuel hyperbole.

But somewhere in our psychology, and certainly somewhere in our culture, we respect facts. We think it's sensible to value them and not invent them.

Some people more than others value them, but is it possible that some cultures do more than others? Am I completely off the mark to think that in many parts of the Middle East facts are barely understood, and certainly don't have the position they do in the West?

But wait! Why make claims for the West?

Haven't we recently gone through a period in the US where faith-based reality superseded fact-based reality? Weren't we asked to take Iraqi Weapons of Mass Destruction on faith, or at least on some people's say-so?

And wasn't it the West that spawned the great and awful ideologies of fascist and communist totalitarianism, where all facts became instruments of the state and ended up being nothing more than someone's bellowing claim?

True.

And yet, we look at Arab societies and find what the Dutch-Moroccan scholar Youssef Azghari calls "form-based" thinking. You tell someone not what happened but what he wishes had happened. It is "form" almost in the sense of "good form."

A recent story in the San Francisco Chronicle reports the following:

"Egypt's state-run newspaper Al-Ahram, the nation's oldest, on Friday defended a decision to publish a doctored photograph putting Egypt's president front and center at Mideast peace talks in Washington, saying it was meant to illustrate Hosni Mubarak's key role."

So it's not where he actually stood that counts but where he should have been standing.

Aversion to facts, it seems to me, makes a mockery of logical explanations and promotes conspiracy theories. The Middle East, as is generally known, abounds in conspiracy theories in part because there are so many conspiracies and in larger part because once you've abandoned fact and reason, all you're left with is a conspiracy.

The eighteenth century Enlightenment sought to inculcate in us a love of reason and analysis, and tried to have these replace conspiracy theories as explanations for events. We did not live up to the goals of the Enlightenment but sometimes we try, to the extent that our emotional natures permit.

In personal life we continue to be emotional, but occasionally we correct ourselves. In public life we are often intemperate, but even in these intemperate times some belief in the worth of fact and reason and verifiability persists. It is a value, an ideal, an aspiration, a mindset worth defending against all enemies, foreign and domestic.

2010

Amnesty and the Enduring Question of Immigration

The linguist George Lakoff once wrote that the Republicans were particularly good at framing their issues with the use of catchy words or phrases. Surely "amnesty" is such a word when applied to immigration.

Democrats protest that they're misunderstood in their plans, that that's not what they have in mind, and so one more battle on the same tired old front rages between Left and Right.

Both sides, though, delude themselves.

Does the Right really think that our borders can be sealed or "secured," as they like to say, if only we tried harder, that 2000 miles can be protected with a fence, or electricity, or thousands of police guarding it? All borders are porous, as I know from experience: even during World War Two, some people, myself included—I was seven when my family escaped the Nazi occupiers of Holland, of Belgium, of France—crossed borders illegally, often on foot, and those borders were shorter and more lethally guarded than ours are now.

But does the Left really think that if the present immigration plans are enacted, the immigration "problem" will be solved, that this latest proposal will fix the matter? That this is the war to end all wars? Didn't the Reagan law of 1986 enact pretty much the same thing, a complicated form of, let's just say it, amnesty? It didn't solve anything, except, of course, for the people who then existed undocumented in limbo. But as we all know, a whole new army of would-be residents is here now, and they're the ones who are now in limbo.

A new immigration law, if passed, won't resolve anything for the future. If all the illegals were admitted and legalized this minute, which is far more than some propose, the "immigration problem" would still be the same.

The underlying problem—and I believe it is a problem, though a case can be made that it's not—is that successful countries are a beacon, a shining star, a magnet. Use any metaphor you like, but the United States will not cease to attract those who want a better life, more prosperous, freer, who in effect wish to come here, live here, work here. There will be ebbs and flows, of course, depending in part on the degree of misery in the originating countries, but the flood will never slow, the pressure never end.

Europe is in the same situation. The wars in the Middle East, the wretchedness of almost every country there, the misery of the failed African states, and the relative success of even the poorest European country, create an unending stream of illegal immigrants, refugees, fortune seekers, upwardly striving families, the good and the bad, the just and the unjust.

Many of them spend what little they have to get there; a fearsome number of them die on the way.

As do a fearsome number of our own immigrants. The latest and most heartbreaking wave is that of the children sent by their parents on a frightening, dangerous trip to the US, from such failed Central American states as El Salvador, Honduras and Guatemala. How many die along the way?

We are, of course, luckier in our immigrants than Europe is in theirs. Our influx from Mexico and Central America will assimilate more quickly than Africans into Europe or Muslims from North Africa and the Middle East. Cultural and religious differences make assimilation more difficult, for both sides.

But essentially the problem is the same and not susceptible to remedy. Stable and prosperous countries provoke longing and of necessity beckon irresistibly.

2014

Culture Change—and Culture Clash

What is culture change?

To begin with a trivial example: in the last decade or two, we've been seeing dogs in stores and libraries, even in restaurants, where we had never before encountered them.

How did this minor culture change occur? How did "Disability Assistance Animals," or just "Companion Dogs," become so widely accepted?

One reason is that we pride ourselves on creating a kinder society, and we have, laudably, instituted many supportive measures for disabled people.

We're comfortable with psychological concepts and, where possible, use them. If people need their animals for emotional support, why not?

Inevitably such cultural change brings about political change—legislation, or, in this case, new rules for animals in public places.

Not everyone favors these changes, of course, and many grumble about "political correctness," but on the whole the change is here, probably to stay.

Another small example of culture change: we have become averse to judging people by their appearance. Calling someone "fat" is not done, or not as easily as it was, say, twenty years ago.

Still more important, of course, are the changes having to do with the widespread acceptance of gay people, the generally positive view of intermarriage, the acceptance of alternative lifestyles, including those of gender-fluidity.

Such changes come from complex dynamics within an ever-changing culture.

But now imagine that an outside group insists on changes—Muslims in present-day Europe declaring that their daughters cannot marry anyone of whom the parents don't approve, and imagine that enough Muslims in enough towns in Europe have formed a majority that will actually make any free contact between the sexes almost impossible in that town.

That would be done out of conviction, of course, because this group may feel that the established Western ways are merely a path to decadence, irreligion, and immorality.

Then there will be no slow, gradual change from within: each side will ghettoize its community, and two cultures will live unhappily, uneasily, across a divide. And each side will try to enact by political means what it wants culturally.

But is that not exactly what confronts a devout Christian community in the US, whose members don't accept overall American values of sex and love?

Not quite. The American Christian sect members make an accommodation to the overall society. No such accommodation is made by most in the Muslim ghettoes of Europe. What has happened in those ghettoes is that the populace adheres to a culture far different from that of the dominant society. Various internal political arrangements enforce that difference. Thus the hundreds of "Sharia Councils" in the UK advising Muslims on matters of marriage and divorce already exert an enormous influence and make it difficult for Muslim women to get the sort of justice non-Muslim women do. The Councils are legal, but their decrees frequently go completely against the grain of British custom—and sometimes even British law.

Two competing cultures do not indefinitely exist side by side. Their clash can take many forms. At best, one will try peacefully to change the other. If the dominant culture succeeds in doing so, we call the process "integration."

At worst, the two cultures will live angrily next to one another, alienated and hostile, each trying to change the other, sometimes by force. That is a continuing culture clash.

2016

On Masks and Burkas

I'm fascinated by small changes that happen gradually and are accepted as entirely normal at every step of their evolution. Dogs are now allowed in restaurants if they can be called "service animals." Cigarette smoking has gradually become taboo, though of course—head-scratchingly—marijuana has become more mainstream. Car alarms make noise, and, even in areas of noise abatement, few people complain about them. Hemlines go up and nobody gives much thought to what might once have looked unseemly.

So one of the things to have appeared on the scene that we never saw before is the fully masked man. At one time a feature of burglars and bank robbers, it's now routine apparel of French and German anti-terror police. Other law enforcement officials in many countries also sport this garb. My hunch is that it originated with Palestinian militants who, wanting to remain anonymous, wrapped their faces in their scarves. But wherever it came from, it's here to stay for a while.

The police will say they're masked for a reason: they need to be unrecognizable to terrorists. Well, sure, there's always a reason! But I think the style-change came first, and then a reason for it was given. In the same way, fashion is often explained by way of "comfort."

But far more disturbing than the mask's use for police is its popularity with protestors. Usually, the masked people are violent "anarchists" accompanying peaceful protesters. At the recent riots in Berkeley, these self-described anarchists, their pockets full of rocks and bricks, smashed plate glass windows on campus and in downtown Berkeley. Their vandalism was intense and made worldwide news.

This so-clad "black bloc" has, of course, all kinds of explanations for its attire, though I suppose the desire to blend in with legitimately demonstrating students is paramount. But, as said before, first the style, then the reason for it: this is now the new garb of window smashers.

Evidently dressing up as Batman is legal. But consider this: wearing a burkini on a French beach was for a while not legal. The super-logical French tried to get women out of their burkinis and into skimpy bikinis. Vive la France!

And even stranger, the movement in France, Germany, and, to a lesser extent, the Netherlands, to outlaw the burka, allegedly to allow for facial recognition, is gaining ground at the same time that the mask is becoming part of official law-enforcement dress.

Burkas are said to be against our Western way of life, a symbol of women's degradation, and on the whole detrimental to wearer and onlooker alike.

Probably so. But how "Western" is it for a man to go out in public wearing a mask?

Living with contradictions is of course humanity's fate. But the failure to notice them is what makes homo sapiens a little less "sapient."

2017

World In Turmoil

Christmas Thoughts
on Peace and War

W hat could be more fitting in the holiday season than some reflections on peace and war? Peace is always talked about, longed for, stated as a goal, aspired to as an ideal, and never more so than at the end of the year. But is it really understood? Do people know the causes of peace?

My own view is that people want peace, sure, but they want it so much on their own terms that, in effect, they don't really want it. Meaning that they're so intent on getting their own way they're far readier for war than they know—ready for hurt, anger, hostility.

Similarly, when nations cannot accept feeling thwarted, diplomacy fails and peace falters.

As evidence, here are a few perspectives based partly on the war in Iraq.

1) Despite the lust for planning, rehearsing, and "gaming" possible scenarios, and despite this having been a war of choice, the decision to go to war was emotional rather than rational. The president and his people just wanted to.

2) This war has failed, at least in part, because the "deciders" did not really know the enemy. And they did not want to learn. Their eagerness for war made them ignore all manner of expert advice. In international affairs, cultural ignorance, or innocence, or naiveté, is almost always punished.

3) However flimsy the reasons for going to any war, many people will support it. The joy in a good fight is so great, the expectation of a kind of emotional cleansing so strong, that many people will lose all scruples in the face of it.

4) Once a war is launched, its pleasures and excitements—at least initially—will inflame even peaceful people. That will change only when the war goes badly. *Then* peace becomes ardently desired.

5) How is peace created and maintained? By tolerating dissatisfactions and making endless attempts to adjust one's desires to the exigencies of other people's, or other countries', realities. Peace is often not a happy-making condition—in fact, peace often feels cowardly.

"Why have an army if you can't use it?" famously asked President Clinton's secretary of state, Madeleine Albright, of then-chief of staff General Colin Powell. (Contrary to their present anti-war utterances, a few years later both Albright and former UN ambassador Richard Holbrooke waffled when Bush started promoting his Iraq war.)

6) Diplomacy is widely misunderstood. It's not only a process of endless hairsplitting and hammering out of agreements, which may or may not hold, but it also requires dissembling, flattery, ego building, and bribery.

Henry Kissinger is alleged to have relayed the Israelis' great admiration for the Syrians, and vice-versa, when he created the Golan Heights agreement. That agreement has now held for over thirty-five years.

In the public arena, as well as the personal, emotional bonds, ties, vanities, or embroilments often trump self-interest. For that reason alone, President Bush and Secretary of State Condoleezza Rice should answer the letters of Iran's President Ahmadinejad. Such a correspondence could create opportunities for forging these bonds.

Would wise, peace-loving leaders ignore such opportunities?

2006

Bleak Thoughts on the First Decade: Reflections and Predictions

The suicide bomber is the new and most dangerous weapon of the twenty-first century. Not that it's entirely new or hasn't been used to great effect before, but now it has grown so pervasive that it has made scattered bands of warriors improbably powerful. Asymmetrical warfare is the order of the day. Good defenses are rare.

We've seen these human missiles spread from Palestine to the Middle East generally into America and Europe. Where will they turn up next?

Security measures are bound to remain inefficient. The worst security measure is certainly the one we've taken. Adding layers of bureaucracy to existing spy agencies will make us—and have probably made us—less safe. The more organizations are involved, the less likely they are to "connect the dots."

I wrote as much four years ago when I warned that structural solutions, tinkering with organizational systems, never work. Unfortunately that is the solution America always gravitates to.

Just as a suicide bomber can do incalculable damage, so can a small group of determined fanatics. The Jihadist movement is hydra-headed. Afghanistan, then Pakistan, now Yemen. How many really belong to the Taliban in Pakistan? Not many, and yet look at what they have achieved against a large state. I daresay not only the US but India is watching Pakistan with the gravest apprehension. Could it really live with a Taliban-dominated Pakistan next door?

The odd thing for any student of history or human psychology, or even any onlooker, is how deeply unattractive these ideologies truly are. They preach a lack of freedom, and they practice the destruction of pleasure. Their most precious commodity is fear. But some human beings embrace such punitive ideologies with relish.

Like the Puritans in seventeenth-century Europe, or the early twentieth-century communists, they are strong because they live a crazed, passionate dream and regard themselves as the elect. They will use any means necessary. It will all end only when they spend themselves, or some other attractive notion comes along to defeat this one or make it irrelevant.

Until then I fear the most calamitous spreading of the plague. Predictions are hazardous, of course, but I think the next battleground will be Europe.

Face it, Europe is the prize. Fortress America will remain a fortress for a while, except for a 9/11 here or there; but Europe is actually vulnerable to a combination of extremist attack and inner weakness. First terrorism, then an appeal to local sensibilities.

Europeans may well surrender some of their freedoms through the ballot. I'm not speaking, of course, of perfectly assimilated Muslims being elected to high office. These people are loyal and believe in a post-Enlightenment European dream.

I am speaking of large segments of the European population with a heavy Muslim presence voting for the partial adoption of Sharia law, or the institutionalization of local restrictions against women and gays, or the gradual erosion by legal means of other hard-won rights and freedoms. Those might spell the beginning of the end, though, as mentioned before, that curtain of darkness will not last forever either.

But while it lasts, what an intolerably dark time it will be.

2010

A Very Long-Range Prediction

I f you are a very young reader, you'll be able to test in your lifetime whether the following will come true. So please keep this book in a safe place till, shall we say, 2050.

This past year has been my year for making short-term predictions. I foresaw that Putin would grab Crimea, that the Kurds would surge and make themselves indispensable, and that—later on— ISIS would be slowed down, even stopped, by daily airstrikes—and I continue to predict that the US and Iran will inch closer together as time goes on.

I thought that the Jihadists would continue to take over an African country, as they did in 2012 in Mali, especially the area around Timbuktu, though I certainly did not foresee the French intervention there and eventual victory over the radicals.

The battle for Africa has just begun. At one time I thought Jihadists might try to take over Niger next, possibly aiming for something larger, but I no longer think so: I now think they're aiming for something larger, and far more ominous: Boku Haram is expanding from Nigeria into many countries, and rather than take over one, they may well have in mind to grab several. This is years away, but a very unhappy prospect for many African countries.

It would not surprise me if some US-led coalition will be formed in the coming years to try to stop them, though air strikes would be harder and less successful in the jungle and savannah than in the desert.

That is some years off, but the next predictions are even longer-range.

While ISIS may suffer defeat in Iraq and Syria, I'm by no means predicting that the Islamic State will be destroyed. In some form or other, it will become more powerful. In the great Sunni-Shia war to come, ISIS will be part of a major Sunni alliance, which I think will inevitably be victorious over the Shia. This, I realize, is almost unthinkable for us in the West. And I daresay that the following is almost unthinkable in Israel, but as a consequence of this war, I don't doubt that the Kurds and the Iranians will eventually form an uneasy alliance with Israel. Whether that alliance can save these three countries remains to be seen.

If I'm right, and the Sunnis win, they will not be content with the Middle East. My next long-range prediction owes something to the ideas of the historian Glenn Young, who has argued that Jihadism, Islamic fundamentalism and Islamist extremism are all forms of anti-modernism, that the new battle of the 21st century is simply that of fundamentalism against liberalism, religion against secularism, belief against modernism. The poor, the disaffected, the angry, the anti-decadents, those who once joined the communists, the fascists, the nationalists, etc., are going to fight under the banner of Islamism. As I understand Young, even non-Muslims might join that cause, though they'll have to convert first.

Unfortunately, the outcome is not assured, the long run does not look good for our side, that of liberal democracy. The idea that liberal democracy will ultimately prevail everywhere is pure nonsense and was pure nonsense when Francis Fukuyama first propounded it in 1992. Keep in mind that after the Arab Spring only Tunisia appears to have chosen the way of secularism and liberal democracy.

The titanic battles of the future will not fail to engulf Europe. Radical Islam, the Sunni version, will attack European institutions, large and small. I'm not at all saying that most Muslim residents of Europe want that, but they may be pushed into it by fanatic minorities around them. Surely the twentieth century has taught us to respect the power of the few. Did the Bolsheviks outnumber the Mensheviks? Definitely not.

If you think this is all pure bullshit, please keep in mind that it came to you free of charge—unlike the various "Strategic Intelligence" newsletters that charge corporations a hefty sum for their monthly shovelfuls.

2015

Terrorism

Stalkers and Terrorists: The Emotional Connection

"Remember, exactly five years ago, we walked to the ocean from your house on that beautiful evening? It was my greatest experience in years."

I scarcely remember the evening, don't know when it was, but remember enough to be sure that we didn't walk to the ocean and may just have talked about it.

My acquaintance was using the language of lovers. After all, lovers heighten their beginnings, suffuse them with possibilities and romance, and if they distort these a bit from the point of view of rosy hindsight, so be it, that's part of their intimacy.

Even parents and children heighten the past. It's a way of saying, "You're deeply important to me." These utterances "sacralize" the bond between them.

But here the context was different: there was no bond to strengthen, certainly not a mutual one. Here the remark was meant to signal a strength of feeling; it sought to create, forcibly, a change in our cool and distant relations and make them warmer, more intense.

And it was a kind of emotional blackmail. Now I was supposed to answer in kind, with a similar emotionality. I would now be forced to feel the intensity. It's what linguists call a "performative" statement—it seeks through words to bring about a new situation, a reconstituted reality.

This exchange is, of course, intrinsically unimportant, and I do not want to load it down with over-interpretation. But it is fascinating for the dynamic it shows. When that dynamic is played out, and its feelings are revealed, they are close to those involved in stalkers and stalking.

I'll go even further. Gestures of this sort, as I now see it, amount to a kind of emotional terrorism.

Terrorists, too, want to be recognized—and they too create a relationship that doesn't exist, or exists only in their minds. Feelings are for them the great facts they insist must be acknowledged. In the process, they forge—in both senses of the word—a relationship.

So the act of terror is a kind of clamor for attention, at the same time that it seeks to create what was there only on one side, in the attacker's psyche.

Terrorists, like stalkers, say in effect, "If you can't notice me *this* way, I'll see to it that you'll notice me *that* way!" Like stalkers, they suffer from being spurned and have now found a way to make themselves visible, inescapable, and emotionally ever-present. You can never again ignore them.

Whether impelled by love or rage, they cannot accept neglect or indifference. There is the same inflated experience of past grievances, the same desire for more connection than exists.

"This is a blow against those who launched the Crusades," say the Jihadists. Sure, but we don't remember the Crusades, barely know about them, and actually couldn't care less. Now, of course, we know; we've been jolted into recognition, aware at last.

The ends of terrorism are not strategic but emotional. Their aim is to redress a balance and create an indelible connection.

The inherent gesture is more than a criminal act, more than a statement, more than a message. Its aim is that of the spurned lover: see me, hear me, feel me; you will never escape me!

Terrorists will continue to stalk us, and give up only when stalkers give up: with the advent of a new passion.

2007

Human Behavior and Foreign Policy: A Parallel

P olitical scientists hate it when people compare human behavior to that of nations. But I feel otherwise. Occasionally, there are striking parallels.

Human beings have an extraordinary capacity to invest certain things with extraordinary importance. When you're in love, few other things matter. When you dislike someone, that dislike is not only with you much of the time, but you advance many reasons to bolster and enlarge it.

When you perceive your self-interest threatened, inevitably you dwell on the threat.

But then, explicably or inexplicably, you lose interest. Your beloved marries someone else (or you marry her). Or the person you dislike leaves town, or his presidential term is finally, thank God, over. Or you now define your self-interest as being threatened by someone else.

These concerns are suddenly forgotten, ignored, "demoted" as preoccupations.

All this we know well enough. It's part of what's laughingly called the human condition.

But, I submit to you, this is what happens in foreign affairs as well. Then it's not a laughing matter but almost a form of collective hysteria.

We went into Vietnam because "vital interests" were at stake. Communism had to be halted somewhere. Remember?

In the Sixties and Seventies lots of people (not just LBJ) claimed we had strategic interests there, insisted we did, and few even in the political science establishment said we didn't.

Even those who never believed in the domino theory felt that the fight against communism made Vietnam an important front line. And what happened? After we pulled out, it suddenly wasn't strategically important anymore. Over a decade before the fall of communism, we abandoned the fort—and weren't overrun.

Nothing much happened (except to the Vietnamese and, alas, the Cambodians).

Something similar may take place after Iraq, even though we do have strategic interests in the Middle East and we didn't in Vietnam.

Am I saying that there are no problems other than those we define as problems?

No, of course not.

I am saying that we consider some problems important, while others just like them are ignored. We consider some crucial and vital to our interests, and a few years later, with little change in the picture, we ignore them.

After we leave Iraq there may be all sorts of chaos there— though perhaps less than anticipated, since we probably are one of many militias and would then be gone—but things will not be much worse for us and probably the world.

There will still be the need to buy oil (but the Iraqis will have the need to sell it)—and there will still be the problem of their possibly exporting terrorism.

It's likely that the victorious Shiites would eliminate Al Qaeda and establish an Iran-style government. How much terrorism does Iran export? It has an obnoxious regime, hostile to us, but there's no evidence whatsoever that they send their agents throughout the Western world.

A nuclear Iran is a problem, sure, but a nuclear Pakistan is a greater problem, for reasons that are obvious (proximity to the Taliban, hostility toward India, presence of many radicals inside Pakistan, instability, etc).

But we define Iran's nuclear potential as a great danger, and we don't talk about Pakistan, because we are friendly with its leader—and hope for the best.

We elevate the status of one and drop consideration of the other. After the regime changes, or we lose interest, the problem is then "demoted" or ignored.

I'm not making some frivolous comment about "having a problem only if you think you do," but making a serious point, based on observation.

You can be sure that after we leave Iraq, you'll hear little about Iraq's "strategic importance."

New problems will then be invested with new significance.

2008

September 11, 2001

As I walked to Taraval Street from my house late Tuesday afternoon, two American flags were out. (There would be many more on Wednesday.) In a bar a few blocks farther on, I could see five men intently watching TV in front of two pool tables. When I got to the restaurant where I thought I would have a quick dinner, the owner and her family were also watching TV. I remained the only diner for the next hour.

On the bus today, an uncharacteristic, almost thoughtful silence prevailed. People read the newspaper or kept quiet.

No one I talk to these days can speak of anything else. That mood some people have almost yearned for—of national unity, closeness, unanimity—is suddenly here. It manifests itself in the volunteering, the donating of blood, the spontaneous attendance at places of worship.

And yet, though the country seems to feel with one heart, it inevitably speaks with many voices. After all, opinions continue to differ radically about what should be done. Suggestions range all the way from "Bomb someone, anyone," on the one extreme, to "We must love everyone alike," on the other.

That is to say, no one really knows what should be done. To pursue the elusive terrorists—as if that hasn't been tried many times—risks a great many innocent civilian casualties. To do nothing is unacceptable.

This is what is so compelling about watching TV. The talking heads, the pundits, the terrorism experts, the former National Security advisers do not have a clue either. They sound as if they're agreeing with each other, and they have even accepted each other's language. Suddenly, for example, everyone is asserting, in almost the same words, that you do not need the sort of proof "you would need in a court of law" to convict the terrorists.

They all call for a strong response, and they all say we must be firm and determined and have a long-range plan.

But when it comes to specifics, to targets, to the nature of the retaliation—or even whether retaliation should be the most important ingredient of our response—they differ and, more important, their language gets fuzzy and abstract, and they just "vague out."

They sound decisive and clear, but they aren't. Even the ones who predicted a major terrorist attack on the United States got some of it wrong, since they connected that predicted event to the likely use of biological weapons.

It is hard to blame them. A certain logic has slipped away from attack and counterattack. At one time, terrorism seemed to have a purpose: it softened the victims, made them lose heart. This is different. Can the terrorists really think that now America will change its policies? Last Tuesday's assault seems motivated by revenge, the desire to inflict pain—nothing more.

In such a climate, few things are clear. No retaliation, no military action—certainly no missile shield—will bring the safety and security we all crave.

It's a pity. The emotional unity of the people, the outpouring of horror and grief, would seem to create an opportunity. But the question remains: an opportunity for what?

2001

The "Message" They Send Is Really About Us

Have you noticed? These days we're all sending messages to each other, usually rather oblique ones. People do; countries do. Are these actually messages? If so, what happens to them?

"Messages" are especially big in accounts of other countries' policies and strategies. A recent L.A. Times story proclaims that Taliban suicide bombers killed many people in Kabul to "send a message" that no matter how effective our offensives may be, and wherever they may be, the Taliban control the country anyway. "Pulling off the attack in central Kabul . . . was designed to send a message that the Taliban are not intimidated by the stepped-up military offensive in the southern city of Marjah . . ." No word on whether the message was returned, replied to, understood, filed away, or what.

This cliché of the "message" is disquieting. It hints at great mastery on the part of our policy makers but, I think, shows just the opposite.

In reality, the message is often the deed itself. The Taliban are doing this, almost obviously, because it furthers their goal. The more Westerners they kill, the more likely a

NATO withdrawal will be. No message, really. It is simply itself. Sometimes, Freud said, a cigar is just a cigar—and sometimes a battle is just another battle.

The reason we call it a message is to satisfy ourselves. We like messages; we like decoding them. Not that the Taliban never send messages, or that we're smarter or more devious than they are, but we always seem to see a message. Their trying to communicate with us somehow satisfies our sense of how the world works.

And especially it satisfies the decoders, the analysts, the Think-Tankers, the State Department paper writers and shufflers, the memo masters at the Pentagon, the desk-bound Intel bureaucrats, and of course the cliché-spouters in the media. What they lack in understanding, they gain in self-importance. Some in these outfits may well be first-rate scholars, but, sadly, most are not.

We employ hordes of these people, of varying capacity, and we do so, once again, because their sort of thinking is recognizable and familiar to us. We know them, we're comfortable with them, and they give us the illusion of doing something.

The people who kill civilians with suicide-bombers in order to gain their strategic ends remain distasteful and remote, and must be made more familiar by seeming "to send a message."

So much for Know Thine Enemy.

But despite our regrettable myopia, or self-centeredness, or even obtuseness, I can't help but see something heartening in our trying to find messages. It says to me that words and signals are our bias, that thinking and talking remain our value far more than killing—that discussion is what we favor over annihilation, and that somehow, naively or not, we like to think that compromise with fanatic enemies is ultimately attainable. This may prove untrue, but it's still a belief worth noting and honoring.

2010

In the Wake of the
Paris Attacks

Certain topics always surface in the wake of any terrorist attack in Europe. What stands in the way of Middle Eastern immigrants' assimilation? Inevitably, their high unemployment is cited, or, in the case of France, their almost complete segregation in the inhospitable suburbs of Paris. This and other such subjects are often misunderstood.

Assimilation depends largely on two things: the willingness of the host country to accept the newcomers, and the willingness of the immigrants to integrate into the culture of their new country. Both are needed for large-scale success. Some argue that over time all immigrants, whether wanted or not, find their place, but this, while true for some, is not true for all.

European countries have been reluctant to look at Middle Easterners as happy future members of the family, and, equally damaging, many newcomers have resisted seeing themselves or their children as potentially or actually "French," or "Dutch," or "German."

So to argue that if one side or the other were more forthcoming, assimilation would inevitably happen, is inaccurate. Both sides must be eager, or at least willing.

Note too that Middle Easterners and North Africans cannot possibly have the same desire to be French or German or English as other Europeans migrating into a different European country. For that, the two cultures are just too different. If you come from a related, compatible culture, you will be a much happier immigrant.

Here is where a big confusion arose after Paris. The terrorists were said to be "French," or "Belgian." No, only by nationality. They were free to travel around because they had Belgian or French passports, but they were second or third generation Moroccan-French or Algerian-Belgian and were either kept out of French society or kept themselves out, or both.

This has everything to do with the recent refugee debate. Sure, most of them want to work, lead a good life in Germany or England or the US, but some will inevitably become alienated and be more susceptible to radicalization than any other group. To say they too flee ISIS is not only dishonest (they flee Assad, bombs, war!) but also has no predictive value about their future integration into the West.

Finally, and perhaps controversially: the dream of a genuinely multicultural society is not only illusory but exactly what we should NOT wish for. Of course there's nothing wrong with immigrants speaking their own language, eating their own kind of food, or adhering to their own traditions; but truly multicultural societies with clashing values fall or break apart. Most countries have a dominant culture, with a dominant language (despite

Switzerland), and a dominant set of beliefs. If you don't subscribe to them, you have not assimilated.

Partly a matter of definition, but I contend that the US is not a multicultural country. Despite our great ethnic diversity and formidable political differences, we mostly adhere to (or aspire to) very similar values and beliefs: equality of men and women, worth of the individual, tolerance for differences, a generally secular way of life. Those shared cultural values bind us together in a way no multicultural society could.

Good.

2015

What Goes Into Radicalization?—An Imaginary Profile

Of course, there are many paths to being radicalized, but let me create one possible profile. I imagine the following steps, and the following ingredients in someone's radicalization. I'll narrow it down by placing my hypothetical young man in Europe or the US, but not in the Middle East.

Many have described this young man as ordinary, normal, well adjusted, but profoundly hidden in him is a deep, smoldering resentment, not at all uncommon in adolescents or young adults. Somehow it has become unmistakably clear to him that life has dealt him a bad turn. So glaring was the difference between his own sense of uniqueness and his actual reality that he gradually realized he had to do something important about it, take a radical step, surprise those who thought him plain or took him for granted.

After a brief flirtation with the mosque, and, more important, following a few probes on the Internet where he read inflammatory texts, and watched a few hot-headed preachers, he was now in possession of a glorious secret. Like a man in a new love affair, or even better, like a man with a secret lover (she's married! Or, her parents disapprove! Or, she's much older!), he is possessed of something that makes him happy, glamorous, and yet unable to share with the world. Not only about-to-be radicalized people enjoy their secret; just wanting to have a secret may well be a strong motive for marital infidelity.

But a secret needs to be revealed, either confided to a friend or acted on. He is now ready to come out with it and thereby surprise the world. People will not only see there's more to him than they imagined, they will also realize he is infinitely smarter, more prescient, braver, more original than they thought. They will be impressed by the depth of his thinking. His is the joy of someone who develops a conspiracy theory—surely no one else sees what he sees, nor analyzes as he does: he now understands, for instance, that Extremists Aren't Extreme, and Radicals Have It Right.

Our hypothetical young man has another great pleasure: he can bypass normalcy —college, a job, a conventional family. He is both poet and criminal; like the latter, instead of getting a job, he gets a gun. That way, he can hold up the store rather than work in it. In five minutes he gets done what others take a year of drudgery to accomplish. It's something that underlies much criminal behavior: you skip over the system, you cut through the advice of elders, you jump over the obstacles. Instant riches. The overlap between criminality and radicalism has become abundantly clear of late.

And best of all, what you do isn't wrong but actually right. You're taking your revenge; you're setting right what the world has done to you. If it requires violence, so be it;

that's not wrong either, because it serves a greater good. Justified violence, he ponders, isn't violence.

Our young man sees himself as a winner; he and a few chosen others are surrounded by an ocean of losers.

2016

The Rabbi and the Terrorist

S ome time ago, a rabbi in Israel decreed that married
couples whose "ketubah" (wedding certificate) was
burned in major fires then sweeping over Northern
Israel should cease living together until their document
could be replaced. His idea, as I understand it, was that
without such written proof of marriage, a couple is not
really married.

To me, it's a perfect illustration of the cast of mind that
afflicts fundamentalist religious belief. All religions with
sacred written texts, and many laws and codes explaining
and enforcing these texts, have their militantly literalist
advocates. If you argued with this rabbi that surely
marriage transcends his particular understanding of it —
or transcends the possession of an undamaged wedding
certificate—he would doubtless counter that *your* various
interpretations so dilute the written commandments about
marriage, that the next step would simply be that marriage
could be legal without any ketubah, and the last step surely
would be that any couple just proclaiming their love could
then say they were "married."

Literalists feel that interpretation of a written text suffers
from two major weaknesses: (1) you can make of the text

whatever you want, and (2) the act of interpreting puts the emphasis not on the text but on yourself. So ultimately, they argue, you have changed God's word into your own desire. To the truly devout, interpretation and accommodation are the path to heresy and treason.

I take my major example from Judaism, but my readers will understand that similar observations apply to Christianity and Islam. In fact, similar observations about text and interpretation can be made about "strict constructionists" of the Constitution — "originalists" —as opposed to those who see the constitution as the proverbial "living, breathing" thing.

Islam, of course, has its large share of clerical literalists. But one problem we all have to contend with nowadays is that it's not only the imams and their zealous followers who have this mindset but terrorists as well. To them, all discussion, all assimilation, all adaptation, is a form of heresy. Only Jihad, as they define it, is pure. The way they "serve" Allah is in the way we have seen in London, Paris, Nice, Berlin, Orlando and San Bernardino. Being in the land of infidels, they find a wealth of targets, in that the whole nation is perceived as the enemy of their faith.

Everything they see—the shops with their mannequins— TV commercials—the great varieties of secularism in all facets of life—all look like unbelief and hedonism. They see God defied and desecrated at every corner. When they commit one of their atrocities, they feel they have struck a blow in Allah's defense.

Where historians have occasionally spoken of the great emptiness created by the decline of religion in the West, or the lack of emotional sustenance that the secular life has wrought, or the difficulty of creating values that are not sanctified by God, the terrorists see a simple remedy for a simple void: strike down the intruders, nullify the fake spirituality of those who love God only conditionally or not at all, and eradicate people who choose to set themselves up as the masters of their own belief.

It's a way of thinking that the rabbi could well understand. But there is one great difference: the hard line of the terrorist tends to be freshly acquired, like that of the convert, who finds in this absolutism a perfect fit for assuaging his failures, his frustrations, and fulfilling his search for identity and meaning. Hence the commonness of European-born terrorists, with good French or Dutch or German, and poor Arabic. Their new-found dogmatism combines the zealotry of the convert with the rage of the self-defined victim who finally seizes the chance to lash back.

2017

Recent Past: Accommodation and Extremism

Death of Pim Fortuyn: End of the Great Dutch Social Experiment?

W hen the first Dutch politician in three hundred years to be assassinated lay dead last spring, people in the Netherlands were saying that everything had changed.

But the huge popularity of the murdered Pim Fortuyn was itself a sign that everything had changed. He was a photogenic, well-spoken, flamboyantly gay man who openly questioned his government's policies on immigration and derided the Establishment's condescension toward ordinary people. He never disguised his homosexuality and even joked about it. Nevertheless, Fortuyn had started to draw huge crowds and win local elections.

Attacked by the Dutch ruling coalition as a right-winger, a Dutch Le Pen, a homegrown Haider, Fortuyn was none of these. He was a populist with an occasionally confusing message but a style of saying things and asking questions that was forceful, challenging and frequently colorful.

He asked, for example, whether a huge Muslim population, often originating in isolated North African villages, could live within the norms of a tolerant, secular, democratic society when powerful Muslim religious leaders attacked homosexuals as deserving of the death penalty.

And he raised the question heretofore posed publicly only by right-wingers, but privately by millions of Dutch people, whether the Netherlands was "full." Can a tiny country with sixteen million inhabitants support more immigrants, more asylum seekers, more migrants? Is such growth possible? Is it culturally sustainable? The non-Dutch inhabitants now number close to two million, roughly 12 percent of the total population.

"He said what we thought," many people said after the death of their hero. The established parties had failed to notice the growing alarm of the population about minority crime or the abuse of the dole (more than half of the immigrant community is supported by the state). They spoke their abstract, politically correct language, retreated to their safe enclaves, and thought of crime as a statistic. The respectable newspapers too did not want to look reactionary; after all, Holland was famously a liberal, tolerant society.

Pim Fortuyn did not live to see any of his questions answered—or even posed by elected politicians. After his death, though, his party of loosely affiliated, hastily assembled candidates became the second largest bloc elected to the Parliament in The Hague.

Their performance in power was a huge disappointment—they were aggressive, but mainly toward each other. Their ineptitude and quarrelsomeness caused the collapse of the coalition government in which they served. And in a new election, they were soundly defeated.

Still, Fortuyn's accomplishment is that these days everything can be talked about. Political correctness is dead. Immigrants are now required to learn the Dutch language and made to study the ways of a secular, tolerant society, in which laws and institutions are supreme and all religions equally protected.

How successful those legal mandates will be is an open question. The immigrants will have to want to integrate, and the Dutch will have to be more forthcoming about recognizing them as "fully Dutch." The outcome of both remains to be seen.

And now that the most recently held elections have returned the established parties to power, can we be sure these parties will not resume the policies of silence and political correctness they were widely accused of fostering?

Many questions are still unresolved. If the country has indeed swung to the right, what now of the legendarily tolerant marijuana laws, homosexual marriages, the semi-legalized assisted suicides? Are we to assume that they will endure now that everything else has changed?

Or is the great social experiment of the last fifty years over?

2003

European Anger: Fighting the Wrong Battle

By widely reprinting the Danish cartoons of Muhammad, Europeans are finally taking a stand— but for the wrong reason, on the wrong issue, and probably at the wrong time.

Why now?

Divorce lawyers call it "the waffle iron syndrome." The couple is divorcing; everything is being quietly and amicably divided. She gets the house, he gets the cash; the books are clearly hers, but the CD collection goes to him.

It all proceeds this way for a while till she says, "I'll take the waffle iron. Okay?"

He retorts, "You'll take *what*?"

And they have the biggest fight ever.

Even without a divorce, every couple has been there. Quiet and restraint and decorum prevail, grievances are ignored or swallowed, till somebody has a major tantrum— usually about the wrong thing, at the wrong time.

For decades, Western European elites, governmental and otherwise, have been so quiet, so discreet, so politically correct, that until the upheavals of the last few years (the murder of Theo van Gogh in the Netherlands and the riots in France), no criticism of Muslim immigrants could be expressed in polite company. Those who did so were labeled racists or far-Rightists, or even neo-Nazis.

But then the dam burst, and now many polite Europeans are having a tantrum. Recent cartoon-inspired violence may worsen it.

It's hard to exaggerate the reproaches against politicians, journalists, educators, and other movers and shakers for having swept immigrant problems under the rug, for keeping silent in the face of problems with integration, or no integration at all. The scorn, ridicule and fury directed against those who should have spoken up but didn't, or hypocritically moved away from immigrant-heavy, crime-ridden city centers, or sent their kids to "good" schools, was not widely reported in the US press. In Denmark, the Netherlands, Belgium, and Sweden, the reproaches continue to this day.

Now it's all out in the open. No More Silence; No More Political Correctness.

Suddenly, many Europeans find the complaints of Muslims about newspaper cartoons first published in Denmark's *Jyllands Posten* (for instance, of the Prophet as terrorist) unacceptable. The furious response by Muslims could harden those feelings.

As if to make up for lost time, and not content to let Danes and their Muslim immigrants work things out, newspapers in France, Germany, the Netherlands, Switzerland, Spain, and Italy have now reprinted the offending cartoons. You don't have to be a Muslim to see that as a clear case of provocation.

And certainly the wrong battle about the wrong issue.

People who passed over in silence the suggestion of some imams that homosexuals should be flung from the tops of tall buildings now take umbrage at Muslim rage about offensive cartoons. People who had allowed plays to be withdrawn because they offended Muslim sensibilities now decry Muslim inability to understand that freedom means freedom to insult. People who had said "immigrants just needed more time to adjust" are now beside themselves about Muslim fury at having their Prophet caricatured.

Yes, freedom of the press is an important value, to be sure, but you can't exactly blame Muslims for being angry. And while Europe does not have precisely the same definition of "hate-speech" we do, it's not as if that concept is unknown there. After all, Holocaust-denial is a crime in several European countries.

Besides, ask yourself if anti-Jewish caricatures would have been widely reprinted in major European newspapers. Democracies, we should know, must treat their minorities with kid gloves. The dominant culture is by definition sturdier than any number of minority cultures. For reasons that should be obvious, an American university can have a black studies program but not a white studies program. That's not a double standard.

The two sides, says the Dutch Moroccan scholar Youssef Azghari, "still don't know much about each other."

The burning of the Danish and Norwegian embassies in Damascus, and the riots and demonstrations elsewhere, make this harder—but, still, now is the time to learn, and for Europeans to show the understanding that in their time of silence and quietude they seemed to demonstrate so excessively.

No point going from one extreme to the other.

2006

Europe Emboldens Its Muslim Women

Recently, the Bangladeshi banker Muhammad Yunus won the Nobel Peace Prize for having pioneered the granting of small loans to new enterprises. Most of his clients are women. What is well known to lenders, foreign aid agencies, and donors generally, but less so to the general public, is that huge numbers of the Third World's small entrepreneurs are women.

A worldwide but underreported phenomenon is that, when given the chance, women are more enterprising, more flexible, and more adaptable than men in adjusting to new ways and rising in an environment that often remains alien to men. In the developing world, it's often women who support the family by running a small business or otherwise providing a stable income. Certainly they're the ones grasping new opportunities.

A similar pattern is at work among immigrants into developed countries. Take the case of Muslim women in Western Europe.

An essay on Moroccan women in the Netherlands makes the point that they're less likely to want to return to their homelands than Moroccan men. It's not hard to understand—by returning, they have more to lose.

One of the untold stories of the immigration turmoil in Western Europe is that such women, despite their lesser position in the family—maybe because of it—do better in Europe than Muslim men. Compared to their powerlessness and isolation back home, they have freedoms and opportunities undreamt of before.

The reason they're not much in the news is that most Muslim women in Europe are quietly functioning as homemakers or as workers in a variety of jobs outside the home.

And their daughters and granddaughters, the second and third generation born in Europe, tend to do better in school than their sons and grandsons. This has been consistently so, though there are danger signs on the horizon. A French high-school teacher told me that some girls are starting to model themselves on the boys and flirt with negative, rejectionist attitudes. But most Muslim girls, she conceded, continue to perform better.

One reason, says the Moroccan Dutch scholar Youssef Azghari, is that girls are more strictly brought up and closely watched. Doing homework, studying, and preparing for a profession comes more easily to them than to boys, who are allowed to hang out on the street till all hours.

Whether it's that boys are more indulged, or fall prey to gangs, or simply don't respond as well to hardships, is difficult to say; but, on the whole, girls adjust and even find European ways compatible with their own lives and see opportunities that boys do not.

Maybe it's that girls expect greater pressure and have learned to be so pliable—to juggle stern fathers and difficult brothers—that anything European society can throw at them is easy compared to what they've already learned to put up with at home, from their own culture, in their own circle.

Obviously, in their behavior and their beliefs, these are the moderate Muslims that native Europeans clamor and yearn for. Why, then, aren't they appreciated more?

Because they're largely unseen and make no waves.

Of course, there are famous Muslim women in Europe, such as Ayaan Hirsi Ali, the Somali-born former member of the Dutch Parliament, now at the American Enterprise Institute in Washington. Her books, her outspokenness against her former religion, her film script of *Submission*— the ill-fated documentary that in 2004 occasioned the murder of its director Theo van Gogh by a radicalized young Dutch-born Muslim—have been publicized all over the world, but her stridency and her rejection of Islam are not shared by most Muslim women in Western Europe.

Nor do most Muslim women sympathize with the other extreme—fanatical devotion to the faith, or fundamentalist radicalism.

When Muslim women are well known, it's usually not because they've thrown over their religion or, at the other extreme, joined a radical group, but because they achieve prominence in approved-of, conventional ways. Six Muslim women hold seats in the Dutch Parliament, as compared to three Muslim men.

Radical groups and furious rhetoric apparently have less appeal to women. A young man may fall into the hands of a radical gang or be dazzled by a fiery imam, in large part because of a certain attraction to an exotic, subversive style. Heavy-handed, high-flown, sternly patriarchal language heard in mosques and on satellite TV, whether as political pronouncement, sacred text, or bombastic invective, may cast the spell of righteous, moralistic exhortation over men, but sways fewer women who, after all, have had such language used against them by their fathers and brothers. Familiar as it is, they fear it.

Similarly, ghetto speech, street language, whether utilitarian or rap-like, induces no great admiration. And young women may be more sensitive to the rage it provokes in the respectable European classes around them. An example of this rage is manifest in the French philosopher Alain Finkielkraut's characterization of such speech as "simplistic, vicious pidgin, pathetically hostile to beauty and nuance."

In her novel *Kiffe Kiffe Tomorrow*, the young Algerian-French writer Faiza Guène shows her imperviousness to these flights of extremist fancy. Instead, the young girl who is the main character appreciates her mother's energy, common sense, and persistence. The mother has a job and is learning to read and write French. Fortunately, the father has long since returned to North Africa to live with a younger woman.

The phenomenon of absent fathers may actually have helped many a young Muslim woman. Fatherlessness permits the new culture to be more accessible. The lessening pressure also makes competing with boys in school more respectable and, as the Dutch sociologist Abram de Swaan has pointed out, education changes the relation of young Muslim women to Muslim men. Small wonder that ever more Muslim women graduate from European universities.

In the Netherlands and Belgium, a good many women of North African and Middle Eastern descent are succeeding as psychologists, social workers, and counselors, thereby demonstrating that, while more needs to be done on all sides, assimilation and success in the new society are both desirable and possible, and even now within reach.

2006

Complexities of Integrating Muslims into Europe

The debate about immigration in the U.S., whatever its complications, is relatively straightforward compared to that raging in Europe, where complexities of policy, attitude toward outsiders and the nature of immigrants' backgrounds dominate all discussions.

During a teaching stint at the University of Helsinki in the early nineties, I was at a dinner party where the inevitable subject of immigration came up. Finland had recently taken in two thousand Somalis and resisted admitting more. It discouraged immigration and has remained homogeneous ever since.

Sweden, on the other hand, was much easier about giving political asylum and had hundreds of thousands of Muslim immigrants already. Now it has more.

The academics around the table wished Finland would be more like Sweden in this regard. My comment that some day Finland might be spared many problems was treated with polite silence—as was a remark from the other extreme by another guest, that he wouldn't mind a million or two Russians "who'd liven things up in Finland" (at that time, it was widely rumored that hungry Russians would soon swarm across Finnish borders).

Finland vs. Sweden is only one of many contrasts in the way European countries have handled immigration. These days, the usual contrast is between Sweden and Denmark. Denmark has taken a hard line with its Muslims, restricting further immigration in part by clamping down on marriage between resident Muslims and the spouse they might send for in the home country. Sweden, on the other hand, remains almost aggressively lenient.

Sharp differences about integration and assimilation of immigrant and minority populations into Europe continue to exist.

There is the French model of integration—dented somewhat by last year's immigrant riots in the notorious ghetto-like suburbs—that everybody living in France should be French, period, while the British multicultural model attempts to avoid segregated suburban high-rises and encourages immigrants to retain their own culture. Of course, in practice the two models frequently overlap.

In fact, within France, many variations exist: Paris favors the "be French" model, while Marseille—a Mediterranean city with vast experience of non-French residents—has gone in for a more multicultural system, less segregation, and greater flexibility in having Muslims play a significant role in the civic life of the city.

The Netherlands has tried both models, especially in housing. At certain times, urban planning produced ghettoization, at other times greater mingling. Despite many pronouncements, neither has worked well. The last five years—after the rise and fall of populist politician Pim Fortuyn and the murder of filmmaker Theo van Gogh—have ended the silence and quieted politically correct platitudes, and the country has almost swung the other way, towards overt anger, pessimism and despair. Moderate native and Muslim Dutch voices are now often going unheard.

As if these complications weren't enough, let it be noted that there are major differences between Muslim immigrant groups. Algerians in France, Moroccans in the Netherlands, Turks in Germany, Iraqis in Scandinavia may all be Muslim, but their cultural backgrounds differ. Add to that the hostility between minorities within minorities: recently the Dutch newspaper *NRC Handelsblad* reported on a group of Syrian Christians in the Dutch town of Enschede who were collectively accused of hooliganism. As it turned out, an unsympathetic Turkish Dutch Muslim city councilman was the main complainant about what most townspeople saw as an exemplary subgroup.

Any number of Muslim immigrants function well as Dutch citizens, but the country's attention appears focused on criminal Moroccan youth, especially in the big cities, and the potential for terrorism among seemingly assimilated but radicalized youngsters, often of school age.

In a country of sixteen million, over a million Muslims, mainly of Turkish and Moroccan descent, now dominate the debate. How best to integrate them? Do they even want to integrate? Can a large minority refuse to integrate?

In his meteoric career, the populist Pim Fortuyn proposed that no country could be truly multicultural without fragmenting. Pluralist, yes; multiculturalist, not really.

This may well contain the key to the present dilemma. Muslim groups, which see their culture as entirely the equal of the prevailing Dutch culture, may be on a collision course with the host country. Norms of free speech and the equality of women, the Dutch now say, are not negotiable. The dominant culture has to be respected and in some fashion submitted to by all the citizens. The fabled Dutch tolerance cannot yield to those who are intolerant of its major values.

This would seem to be the advice of a recent book, *While Europe Slept*, which dwells on the habitual looking away of liberal European elites, a silence it regards as continuing. The author, Bruce Bawer, claims that if Europe does not defend against its "Weimar Moment," it will be destroyed from within. The Weimar Republic, it should be recalled, failed to take a stand against Hitler's extremism before he came to power.

But, as Bawer also notes, not only will the European Establishments have to come down hard on extremist behavior and even thought, they will also have to guarantee full equality to their newly minted citizens. For the one thing all European countries have in common is that they never really conceived of the immigrants and their descendants as being truly, really, genuinely Dutch or French or Danish or Swedish. That is a major difference between these countries and the US.

Immigrants will have to accept the reigning norms—but European host countries need to offer true acceptance and equality. If, in fact, both sides don't change, all will indeed be lost.

2006

Muslims in Europe: Yet Another Dilemma—Or a Passing Phase?

T wo incidents described in a recent issue of the Dutch newspaper *NRC Handelsblad* illustrate one of many dilemmas European society faces these days.

A young Muslim woman, Samira Dahri, a lecturer in economics at a private college in the Netherlands, refused to shake hands with her male associates on religious grounds. When she was dismissed from her job, she took the matter to court, charging that she was being intimidated. "I experience shaking hands," she alleged, "as an undesired form of intimacy, as sexual intimidation."

While the court upheld her dismissal, it would not go so far as to oblige students and staff always to shake hands.

A second incident took place at the Embassy of the Netherlands in Amman, Jordan.

A traveling Member of the Dutch Parliament, Harry van Bommel, said at an embassy lunch to a young Jordanian embassy employee, "You look sensational." She filed a charge with the Dutch ambassador about these "unwanted intimacies."

When the MP noticed that his remark went over badly, he apologized at once. Since then he has offered another, more formal public apology.

The noted Dutch Arabist Rob Ermers, author of a recent book on honor and revenge in the Middle East, analyzed the incident this way:

While it's not forbidden to compliment an Arab woman, the word "sensational" carries sexual overtones and is perhaps close enough to the word "sexual" to have imputed seductive qualities to her.

For her to pass over this, especially since others heard the comment, explains Ermers, might well create the appearance that she was responsive to a suggestive invitation, surely a dishonor to her.

Van Bommel's first apology, continues Ermers, was insufficient because uttered out of earshot of the others at the table. Only a public apology could clear her of having seemed receptive to any overture.

Ermers gives the MP high marks for cultural sensitivity in not reiterating or explaining his innocent intention. Van Bommel apparently realized that the facts were less important than the young woman's honor.

Admirable though Ermers' analysis is, it does not fully persuade me.

Why was this apparently prim young woman, so keenly aware of her honor, at a mixed lunch? And since she was, didn't she have some responsibility to yield to Dutch rather than Arab ways? After all, she was at the Dutch Embassy.

Though Ermers says that filing a complaint was her way of going public, it strikes me as a European (or American) and not exactly Arab thing to do.

As for the woman in the Netherlands who was fired for refusing to shake hands and who charged sexual intimidation, was she not using feminism's hard-won legal techniques to uphold a distinctly non-feminist way of life?

Are such terms and concepts as "hostile workplace" and "unwanted attentions," which would seem to have little legal weight in most Arab Muslim societies, now deployed against the societies that brought such concepts into being— and in favor of values inimical to them?

The paradox is dizzying: Western techniques at the service of non-Western principles, Western means to non-Western ends. And the dilemma for present-day Europe seems to be, can its legal system be used against itself?

But that may be putting the matter too starkly. These two legal challenges could be atypical, and, for that matter, such legalistic probes may be little more than specific responses to perceived general injustices against all Muslims. If so, then this might all be a passing phase, inevitably giving way to yet another passing phase in the larger drama of Muslims in contemporary Europe.

2007

Present Decade: Moderation and Stridency

What About the Moderate Muslims?

After each terrorist attack in Europe, we hear that the majority of Muslims are peace-loving and moderate. True enough. But most people have no idea what pressures these moderates are under.

Many in the European majority population regard the moderates with hostility or suspicion because they're Muslim. And Muslim radicals look at them with anger because moderates are seen as having sold out to unbelievers and their cultures, and will do nothing to advance the cause of Jihad.

I can imagine that the moderates themselves undergo many contradictory emotions: horror at violence, fear of continued rejection—and, not least, a defensive family feeling toward the young radicals, who could be their children or grandchildren or nephews and nieces, and in some cases are. That mixture of feelings is probably the hardest part, since ambivalence, as we all know, is a difficult-to-handle emotion.

After each attack, these moderates are reminded that they must condemn violence unequivocally. Most of them do condemn it, but not unequivocally. And sometimes they're reminded that they must work harder to help the young acculturate in this strange and still new culture of Europe, work they're not equipped to do because they themselves may not be fully acculturated.

But such pressures are small compared to what will face them if (and when?) the radicals gain more power or the number of Muslim immigrants increases. Then family feeling will play a greater role still. After all, the moderates' own allegiance to European culture is often neither particularly solid nor emotionally forged. They may well feel a greater affinity with their country of origin.

Let's take a not-altogether-hypothetical example. If asked whether a given majority Muslim town in Holland or Belgium or France should institute a version of Sharia law, they might vote yes. Their motives are likely once again mixed. Maybe Sharia would keep their own adolescent or grown children in line. Or they might see a personal element in Islamic law as superior to Western law.

At that point their earlier rejection of radicalism seems unimportant, and suddenly moderates will have become less moderate. Faced with a real choice, they might not be able to make a genuine emotional commitment to a culture they're not emotionally committed to.

If they are surrounded by more newcomers of their own religion, to the point where the sheer numbers suggest that their culture should be equal or even dominate the native European culture, then the pressure on the moderates grows even greater. They may be forced to choose in a way that they're not now.

These choices are personal, familial, psychological, cultural, and the results might shock any Westerner. Suppose they're asked to choose between putting more clothes on their daughters or unreservedly defending their daughters' right to wear whatever they want. Are most of them going to choose the "immorality" of letting them walk around "half naked"?

Their choices may well alienate even their friends in European society, the progressives and liberals.

It is this cultural aspect of the matter that's involved in the whole large question of their eventual "integration" into Western society.

At the very least, we should acknowledge that the moderates' future course of action cannot be predicted and their future behavior should not be taken for granted.

2016

Barriers Against Assimilating Europe's Muslims

One of many harrowing scenes during the early days of the latest refugee crisis in Europe occurred when a Syrian father placed his wife and baby on railroad tracks so as to force the authorities to grant his family entry to the train that would take them over a closed border.

Commenting on this in the prominent Dutch newspaper *NRC Handelsblad* (September 15, 2015), the Moroccan-Dutch novelist Hafid Bouazza wrote that Westerners would see the episode as an example of desperation, but he himself regarded it as classic "Arab hysteria," the "mentality" of the Old Testament, with its "sackcloth and ashes and rending of garments."

He noted that the father treated wife and baby as property, adding acidly, "Common enough for Arab children to hear their father say, 'I've made you, and I can unmake you.'"

Those of us who aren't Arabs would feel uneasy using such language about Arabs, or even using words like "hysteria" in this context. But we might, more blandly, say that Arab cultural styles differ from Western, or that "Arab rhetorical modes allow more histrionics." "Mentality" with its overtones of "national character" is now a discredited concept, but "cultural and communicative styles" are respectable terms in our discourse. Translated that way, Hafid Bouazza's comments become less shocking, though their content remains the same.

But even when less harshly formulated, the ways and styles of the "other" are still widely detested. And since styles beget values, and values beget styles, they become potent cultural characteristics, which when they coexist within one land are the source of much tension.

That is the nature of the famous clash of civilizations—a collision of styles, of behavior, of values; two ways of reacting to a problem, two sets of beliefs, two modes of conducting oneself. What we mean by "assimilation" and "integration" is that immigrants choose, by and large, the cultural values of their new country, and that ultimately one dominant culture will prevail there.

Hafid Bouazza himself made that choice, though it was an easy one for a bookish Moroccan kid newly arrived in the Netherlands, who in adolescence discovered he could write exquisite Dutch prose. In fact, Bouazza celebrated his fateful choice in a superb early short story, "Apolline," a love song to a Dutch woman who personified the freedom and opulence of Europe, its exoticism and self-confident sensuality, though also its self-absorption and isolation.

But for other arrivals from the Arab world, no great fondness in either direction, no great cultural affinity. Twenty or thirty or forty years in the West have not necessarily reconciled the two respective cultures or lessened mutual discomfort. There is little affinity between the old culture and the new, despite all the simple-minded warnings, injunctions, and pleas that Europe must "integrate" its Muslims—as if governments hadn't tried and citizens hadn't made the effort.

And there is no guarantee, as many people are now beginning to find out, that even the next generation will easily yield to the styles, the values, the beliefs of their new home. Failing to see the discomfort of disaffinity and the anguish of alienation is to miss the most crucial aspect of the European drama taking place today.

2016

The Silent Majority, the Strident Minority

Since I started writing this series of columns on the assimilation of Muslim immigrants in Europe, I've had much positive response and some negative. Several times I've been chided for not specifying how many people I'm writing about and whether my comments apply to the majority of Muslim immigrants in Europe.

And taken to task for generalizing.

First, the numbers.

A minority often sets the trend. If 40% of all Muslim high school girls in, let us say, Belgium wear the hijab, that's a trend, even if 60% don't, especially if only 5% had done so 25 years ago. And if they take up Koranic studies, and become more devout, then a cultural change may be in the offing.

A trend-setting minority can easily strong-arm or overrule the majority. Were the Puritans a majority in England when they closed the theaters in 1642, a quarter century after Shakespeare's death, and subsequently killed a king, installed a strong man, instituted the religious police, and punished non-church attendance?

The silent majority often yields to the strident minority, depending largely on the fervor of the minority.

As for my generalizing, one objection came from my friend Sheila Gogol, an astute observer of the European scene, who has lived in Amsterdam all her adult life.

"Just like there is very little to be said about 'Christians' or 'Europeans' or 'Americans' because they are each so different and there are so many exceptions to whatever rule you might formulate, there is nothing you can say about 'Muslims'... [Sometimes] you only realize [their identity] when you hear their name. Others act like they never left their picturesque village. Some can barely speak Arabic or Turkish or whatever language their grandparents spoke and have barely ever been inside a mosque. Others stick to the old culture."

And she reminds me pointedly that "from afar, you can develop theories galore..."

A similar objection from my friend Chris Thornton, who has lived and worked in Dubai for a decade and published widely on Middle Eastern affairs. He underscores that Muslims in Europe include "guest workers of the 1970s, children of Palestinian refugees... South Asians in the UK..."

Both of these superbly qualified observers miss the point. It would be foolish to deny the abundant diversity of Muslim immigrants into Europe. Nor would I deny that some Muslims integrate quickly and others do not.

What I try to assess—and generalize about—is the difficulty of the ones who do not. People who integrate poorly belong to a culture that either blocks their integration or makes that integration difficult. Whether secular Syrians or devout North Africans, what values do they adhere to? How do these values interact with local European ones?

As for how we can't generalize about Americans—that's a fallacy.

An art-loving theatre-goer in New York, and a gun-toting Oklahoman father of six, and a biracial, devoutly Christian single mother in Des Moines would seem to have little in common, but not so!

Barring individual psychopathology (or membership in a tiny sect), these Americans, and almost all Americans, subscribe to the idea of human equality, individual self-worth, the benefits of hard work, the superiority of American democracy over other systems. No one would dictate what a spouse must wear, or forbid a daughter to study medicine or shake a man's hand.

Different as they are, they share a culture, its unspoken assumptions and values.

Generalizations not only can be made but must be—by anthropologists, political scientists, cultural studies experts. Would these fields even exist without generalizations?

And generalizations about cultural assimilation figure in the discussion of future cultural change. If an assertive minority of the population turns against crucial Western values, or if a passive majority fails to resist—and reject— the question "Why should we adjust to your values; why don't you adjust to ours?" then the culture will irrevocably change, and not for the better.

2016

"Muslims in Europe": Answer to Some of my Critics

I've had quite a bit of comment from readers about my series of newspaper columns on the subject of Muslims in Europe. Some have asked me why this matter is so much on my mind, and I can only reply that it's probably among the most important events of our time.

I have also had a fair amount of criticism, which on the whole I appreciate greatly. Most writers enjoy being criticized almost as much as praised. It's silence and indifference we can't tolerate.

But there's one bit of criticism I find irksome. When people tell me I'm writing "out of fear," they assume they can be clear-eyed but I can't. For them to say I write out of "fear" is like for me to say they write out of "hope." Why not assume that both of us are as honest as we can be—both of us trying hard to assess what cultural integration in Europe entails in the present and what its future may look like.

Now to more sensible objections:

A frequent question is, why would Muslims in Europe have greater difficulty assimilating into Europe than Italians into late nineteenth or early twentieth century America? Or

East European Jews, or anyone for that matter who came to the US?

The answer I've given in any number of articles, including two that I wrote with the Moroccan-Dutch scholar Youssef Azghari, and are included in this collection, is that Italians or Irish or Jews did not come from a culture entirely different from the new one. Their values, however different, had enough affinity with those of the US to make their assimilation in the second or third generation fairly easy. I have said the same thing about Mexicans entering the US now.

Others have asked me why I don't seem to consider the extremely, fanatically orthodox Jews. I fully agree that those differ from the more secular earlier Jewish immigrants and indeed have much in common with present-day devout Muslims, but the number of Jewish fundamentalists is so small that their assimilation or non-assimilation doesn't count. They are much like the Amish, an interesting but, in this context, insignificant community.

So the question remains: Why a particular difficulty with Muslim integration into European life?

To be sure, there are Turkish Muslims and Moroccan Muslims, Bosnian and Syrian Muslims; some are secular, others not. Some will integrate quickly, others not. The majority will of course assimilate into—i.e., adopt the values of—European life. But a significant minority may well find it almost impossible to do so. They are faced with the specter of integrating into a culture that looks to them as being devoid of culture.

It doesn't make sense to them to assimilate into a void. European cultures appear indistinct, and not even as robustly present as American; the impetus for Muslims to integrate into American culture is of necessity greater.

France may stress its *laicité*, its secular nature, but that just looks like the absence of morality. The Netherlands may highlight its tolerance but that seems merely indifference to things that matter. Italy may put forward its heritage but that resembles paganism in modern dress. At that point a reluctant Muslim may well ask, "Why should we be like you when our way is so much better?"

2016

Well-Meaning Misconceptions about Muslims in Europe

The besetting sin of those of us who are left of center is that we look away from painful realities and turn eagerly to our favorite villains and victims. Add to that the all-too-human tendency to see ourselves as complicated but others as simple—simply oppressed by government, or suffering from someone's incompetence—and you get a brew of false charges and inadequate understanding.

A friend wrote about a recent column of mine on European Muslims that on a visit to the Netherlands she "was shocked to hear that the government of the Netherlands had not tried to integrate these people." Not so: the Dutch government has tried many methods—integration in housing, then its opposite, benign ghettoization, and many more. Each policy seemed to fail after a while; obviously not for everyone, but for many Turks and even more Moroccans.

My friend also wrote that because the government "had not tried to integrate" Muslims, they sent for brides from back home and created their own Islamic schools. Again, this is mistaken. Sending for a bride has nothing to do with what the government does or doesn't do. As for schools, this is no different from American kids going to Catholic school. If other standards are met, no Western government is going to disallow a minority or religious group to have its own schools.

But the major fallacy in such comments is to think that governments can force cultural integration. They can't. They can recommend or initiate policies (e.g., integrated housing, or Affirmative Action in the US, or busing, etc.); they can try to promote integration, but they can't make it happen. Governments cannot force or create assimilation—politics is not culture.

Another critic wrote that she had been in Marseille and was appalled by the huge suburbs with their high-rises full of poor Muslim families. True, but there's more to it. The suburbs were and are full of poor people, but it's wrong to conclude, as she does, that there was "no effort to integrate these people into France or French culture." So many Muslims came so fast to France, and they obviously moved where they could afford to live. Moroccans joined the first wave of Algerians, with the results we know.

Marseille tried not to let it happen that way, since it had an Arab heritage of sorts to begin with and prided itself on being able to manage "its" Muslims better than Paris. On the whole it has. Marseille remains a bit of a model city in France to this day (in contrast to Toulouse!). Inevitably, the high-rises my correspondent saw were full of Arabs, but that is not to say "the government put them there."

Another misconception of many people is to think that Muslims everywhere behave in the same way. Not so. Turks in Germany and Bosnians in Switzerland and Pakistanis in the UK all have different trajectories. Nor can we rule out sudden changes: in the Netherlands it was always said that Turks assimilate more quickly than Moroccans. Just so; but among Turkish youngsters these days, radicalization has suddenly become tempting.

Lately the various generations do not really seem to follow classic immigration patterns. First- and second-generation Pakistanis in Great Britain have integrated well, but third-generation Pakistanis have been more susceptible to radicalization than could have been foreseen. Beautifully assimilated young Belgians, with little Arabic and excellent Dutch or French, have unaccountably taken up the cause of Jihad.

It is precisely the complexity of the subject that many people seem to miss. To say that it is the fault of one side or the other, or of local governments, or of an unwillingness to adapt, or of an unwelcoming attitude, is to distort matters, and to indulge in reflexive and simplistic thinking.

2016

Affinity and Acculturation

Do Arabs Communicate Differently?

At the age of six, Youssef Azghari came to the Netherlands, where his Moroccan father was one of hundreds of thousands of guest workers who wound up staying. Their children comprise a generation marked by radical extremism at one end of the spectrum and flawless integration at the other. Azghari, now thirty-four, is a lecturer in communication and sociology at a Dutch college.

His recent book, *Cultuurbepaalde communicatie* (*Culturally Determined Communication*), not yet translated from the Dutch, draws on his own experience with Moroccans in the Netherlands as well as scholarly analysis—and can tell us much about both the culture clash we see everywhere in Western Europe and the societies in the Muslim world we so eagerly seek to change.

In the Netherlands, the 2004 murder of Dutch filmmaker Theo van Gogh has painfully refocused the struggle to assimilate a substantial Muslim minority.

Before Van Gogh's murder came the assassination of the Dutch populist and anti-immigration politician Pim Fortuyn. And before that came September 11, 2001, which had considerable impact on Holland. The last four years have seen a sharp reversal of that country's widely admired love of tolerance.

Azghari clearly hopes to replace both unquestioning tolerance and wholesale rejection with understanding on both sides. In the process, he offers a fascinating look at what the West doesn't quite grasp in Muslim cultures, and vice versa.

He draws a sharp contrast between the two cultures but knows that there are gradations in between. As he sees it, the Netherlands—the West, really—is a "content-directed" society, by which he means that its societies care more for the content of the message than the form in which it's delivered.

Equality, honesty, acceptance, tolerance, and clarity are values such societies espouse. Even children are urged to think for themselves. Freedom of expression, individualism, and democracy are prized above everything.

The East, which Azghari takes to include the Muslim world as well as much of Asia, is "form-directed." Its societies value the package more than the message, he argues. The way something is said trumps individual expression.

Obedience, loyalty, respect, empathy, and discretion are supreme values. The naked truth is unseemly, for truth is less consequential than the manner in which it is revealed.

Children learn to respect their elders, and citizens learn to fear the state. Such societies ultimately favor a hierarchy, a reigning ideology—and a strong leader. Loyalty counts for more than self, and sacrifice is venerated.

While such observations about West and East are not new, and may well be oversimplified, there is special value in hearing them from someone with such intimate experience of both cultures. And there may be special merit in applying these ideas to the judgments made in the West about the Muslim world and our interventions in the Middle East.

Take, for instance, the idea you sometimes hear from our soldiers in Iraq, that Iraqis "can't be trusted," or "lie" to you.

Azghari argues that several factors can be misinterpreted by Westerners when Arabs are reporting actualities: a certain "poeticizing" tendency, embellishing what is otherwise bald and unpleasant; a desire to spare listeners by telling them what will please them; and an emphasis on intentions rather than results. This lack of factuality has often been observed and derided by Westerners.

While we do not have to take this somewhat over-schematized view as literally as Azghari suggests, it could help clarify for us the world we are now in conflict with.

At least it could temper our optimistic predictions about its democratic future, for despite Turkey and Mali, Muslim societies have shown no great affinity for democracy. Equality and democracy are simply lesser values for them.

Add to that the radicalization Azghari notes in second-generation Muslims in Western Europe, and you can predict both more terrorism in the West and a tumultuous, undemocratic future in Iraq.

2006

Theft and Survival

Books about Islam just keep on coming, and one can only wonder who reads them. The specialist, inevitably; the general reader, maybe. But do our policy makers? Our national debates are conducted—and policies formulated—on the basis of slogans, half-truths, distortions and ignorance.

So knowledge is essential, a point *The Great Theft: Wrestling Islam from the Extremists* underscores. The author, Khaled Abou El Fadl, is a law professor at UCLA who has published ten books on Islam. His specialty is Islamic jurisprudence; but while his book is detailed and occasionally dry, it lucidly answers major questions of Westerners about Islam. Additionally, it implores Muslim moderates to restore Islam to the traditions of inquiry and tolerance that have been stolen from them by extremists—or puritans, as Abou El Fadl prefers to call them—and urges the West to view that schism as comparable to the violent Reformation that once shook Christianity.

The Great Theft explains the origins of modern extremism, its roots in the eighteenth-century reformist Wahhabi movement, and its arguments with mainstream Islam. Both mysticism and rationalism, Abd al-Wahhab preached, as well as intellectualism and sectarianism, had undermined Islam; only a literal return to the Prophet's words, literally interpreted, could restore Islam to itself. Thanks in part to Saudi Arabia's vigorous export of this radical movement, the puritans have eradicated Islam's rich history and now dominate the way the religion is viewed. But, says Abou El Fadl, Islam finds itself in a great "transformative moment"—though the majority moderates have been overshadowed by extremism, they can, with knowledge and understanding, still take Islam back.

One manifestation of extremism is, of course, the notion of Jihad. Even the non-scholar is familiar with the term's two major interpretations: one, that it is essentially a struggle with oneself for a kind of moral self-improvement; the other, that it is a fight to the death against all infidels. Citing Qur'anic chapter and verse, and drawing on Islamic scholarship, Abou El Fadl demonstrates that the latter is a radical misinterpretation of the Prophet and what he stood for. Known to us from Osama bin Laden's various proclamations, this version is especially appealing to those who wish to forge a new identity by defining themselves as heroic followers of the true path.

Similarly, the author argues that it is a puritan perversion of Islam and the Qur'an to treat women as, say, the Taliban does—that in fact Prophet and text plead for a humane and rational treatment of all people, with human worth and dignity transcending all other considerations. He does so with much passion and scholarly exegesis but is most persuasive when he lays bare the sadistic motives beneath the precepts of the puritans.

Still, the uncomfortable question lingers: why, if the Qur'an stresses equality, cooperation, mutual support, and so forth, is the situation of women what it is in so many Muslim families, in so many countries?

Which leads to my one complaint about this otherwise fine, instructive book. It extols the path of moderation, portrayed as the core of Islam, but, despite many reasons given, does not quite manage to say why the theft of Islam was so thorough. Maybe fanaticism always beats out moderation, but in the case of Islam the moderates seem particularly weak. It's fascinating to hear Abou El Fadl explain why Saudi Arabia dare not become more moderate—because as guardian of the holy places it "must define orthodoxy in the Muslim world"—but he does not account fully for the disarray, religious and cultural, of so many more moderate Muslim countries.

These are not matters that *Embracing the Infidel: Stories of Muslim Migrants on the Journey West* deals with. Despite its title, the book is not concerned with the nature of Islam. The author, Behzad Yaghmaian, an Iranian American professor of economics, tells the stories of Muslim migrants, who for one reason or another, have left their homelands. His book is a gripping tale of hardship, adventure, and yearning; of hopes raised and dashed; and of troubled and sometimes heroic adaptations to refugee camps in Bulgaria, tent cities in Greece, slum ghettos in Turkey, and, for the luckier ones, fugitive existences in Paris and London. Whether from the Islamic Republic of Iran or Saddam Hussein's Iraq or post-Taliban Afghanistan, the migrants are bent on survival and a better life in the West.

Their obsession with visas, petitions, passports, documents, and borders reminds me of European Jews before and after the outbreak of World War II. I remember the same rumors about countries that don't send illegal border-crossers back, but actually do (Switzerland, then; Greece, now); the same obstacles, both natural and human— hideous mountain ranges, treacherous people smugglers, predatory and brutal border guards.

But traumatic though the situation of these wanderers is, and though they flee horrendous conditions, their fate if they must return home is not as inevitable as it was for European Jews. Many present-day migrants are not classic "political refugees." Is a woman escaping an oppressive Muslim father a political refugee? Does having your family in Afghanistan wiped out by American bombs earn you political asylum?

One of many strengths of this book is to show how blurry such categories are and what strangely mixed motives impel these brave, complicated people. A masterful storyteller, Yaghmaian reveals many layers to the refugees' personalities and histories, and some to his own. He wins their trust, not because he wants to write a book, but because he becomes deeply enmeshed in their lives.

Difficult as things are for the migrants, they can only become worse: the West now deems Afghanistan and Iraq "safe" to return to, while the fear of terrorism has further tightened Western entry requirements. More will ultimately have to go home.

Perhaps the only silver lining a detached observer might find is that the continued presence of such strong-minded, independent people in their homelands might make more likely the realization of the dream, cherished by the likes of Abou El Fadl, for a more moderate Islamic world.

Manfred Wolf

The Great Theft: Wrestling Islam from the Extremists
by Khaled Abou El Fadl
Harper San Francisco; 320 pages; $21.95

*Embracing the Infidel: Stories of Muslim Migrants on the
Journey West* by Behzad Yaghmaian
Delacorte Press/Bantam Dell Books; 368 pages; $24

2006

Identity and Diversity: Muslims in the US and Europe (with Youssef Azghari)

The European attitude towards immigration is often contrasted with the American. In the US, assimilation is said to be easier, immigrants made to feel more quickly at home (leaving aside, of course, the illegal immigrants streaming in from Mexico). The second and third generation of immigrants are Americans, sometimes "hyphenated" (e.g., Italian-Americans) but still Americans. They're no longer "immigrants," as they are in Europe.

This observation about the US has become a common side bar of the 'Muslims in Europe' debate.

Further, the makeup of America's Muslims is frequently compared favorably to its European counterpart. In the United States, the income of Muslim Americans parallels that of the average American and ranks higher than the income of African Americans or Hispanics. Sometimes prosperous middle-class neighborhoods are pointed to—for instance, the town of Fremont in the San Francisco Bay Area is a rather comfortable suburban settlement of tens of thousands of Afghan Americans who live contentedly in their small-town setting. And while not prosperous, the city of Dearborn, Michigan, numbers tens of thousands of middle class Arab-Americans.

True, once in a while radical activity manifests itself in such far-flung places as Florida or upstate New York, but these can be considered exceptions that prove the rule.

Several reasons for the difference between Europe and the US come to mind. Immigrants came to the US of their own volition. Once the masses swept over Ellis Island in the nineteenth century they had to fend for themselves. The government did not protect them or otherwise care for them. It wished them well, but that was about it. After all, they were not asked to come.

This rather hard attitude toward the newcomer has not gone away—while difficult for some, especially from a group-oriented culture, it actually favored the individualist, the adventurer, the entrepreneur.

Many Muslim immigrants in America have a middle class background and arrived here neither penniless nor illiterate. The differences with Europe are striking, since most Muslims came to Europe either as guest workers or political refugees. The former, of course, were solicited, asked to come to work in European factories. They were ideal for the assembly line and not selected for their brain power. Thus many Moroccans who came to northern Europe were actually Berbers from the Rif Mountains, impoverished and illiterate. The consequence to this day is that European Muslims are socially less prominent and frequently ghettoized.

Another difference between America and Europe in the reception of Muslims brings us closer to the subject of identity. American culture is less circumscribed in what it regards as American behavior. There are many ways to be an American. If Ahmed and Yasmina have jobs, live in a nice house, raise a few reasonably well-behaved children who go to school and don't get into major trouble, then it doesn't diminish their Americanness in the least if they celebrate Ramadan, or go to the mosque—or wear whatever, including a head scarf.

This looseness of what it means to be American goes along with a belief that American culture is powerful enough to overcome other influences and maybe other identities. We know that American fashions, pop culture, the English language will rise to the globalized top.

Considering the pervasiveness of American culture worldwide, that's realistic enough.

There is of course at times a culture clash, a disaffinity between the old and the new—legendary historic quarrels between parents and children—but this appears to smooth itself out in time.

The new identity, precisely because of a certain easy lack of insistence by the prevailing culture, emerges without major birth pangs.

In the large American family with so many odd members, one more odd member won't stick out. In Europe, the family is smaller and more homogeneous, hence more exclusive.

And to stay with the family metaphor: the US can be said to behave like a strict father, urging his children to fend for themselves, be independent, solve their own problems, see to the future. Europe plays the role of the mother, who tries to protect the children, do as much for them as possible, watch over their needs and ward off some of life's problems.

She also has a somewhat narrower view of the values she would like her children to uphold: some behavior is out of bounds. Europe is more restrictive about its identity. America's relative looseness about how to behave—what constitutes an American—allows for easier entry into the society. Norms and values are not as constrained or narrowly defined as they are in Europe.

Perhaps one way of reconciling these two parental attitudes is that the father needs to exercise a little more care and patience, while the mother should show a little more understanding of the children's independence and display greater flexibility about their norms and values.

America could be a little less distant and more caring, Europe less protective and more easygoing.

2007

Young Moroccans in the Netherlands: Crime and Radicalism

I have said repeatedly that not only will immigrants have to bend to European ways, but also Europeans will have to change their notion of what makes a citizen; they will have to become more flexible about what constitutes being Dutch or French or German.

But even with the goodwill of this moderate way, both paths are difficult for both sides. The Dutch cannot simply abandon the feeling that to be Dutch is to be a member of a family, while the immigrants cannot easily leave their cultural ways behind. In my view, theirs is the greater task because they have to accommodate to a new language, a new way of doing things; in short, they have to embrace, however grudgingly, new styles, new mores, new values.

This is why merely teaching immigrants Dutch, testing them on certain political rights and obligations in the new country, however important, is not enough. Even aside from the unpleasantness of the constant hammering reminders— about which the writer Adriaan van Dis once said wittily that it made him want to wear a burka—something is lacking. In order to subscribe fully to the *"rechtsstaat"* or state of laws, you have to do more than subscribe to some of its laws; you have to embrace them and become part of the culture. The latter actually precedes the former. Your beliefs as well as your style have to change first. Thus, to gain a sense of ease in the new society, you cannot retain the belief that honor comes to you from rank or wealth or fidelity to a sacred text, but that you have to earn it, through work, achievement, status gained by way of some kind of accomplishment.

So to be assimilated into the new culture requires on the part of the newcomer cultural change, an adjustment of attitude, an absorption into something strange and new. That some immigrants take to it greedily means only that they, as it were, yearned for such possibilities all their lives. That others accommodate to it moderately well signifies that they have bourgeois aspirations and fit into Western society. The ultimate aim of assimilation, I believe, is for as many immigrants as possible to enter that middle class. Only then can they be said to be fully of the new country.

But isn't this a matter of economics as much as culture?

Certainly—but these economic opportunities and possibilities bring with them a change of style, or are made possible by the change of style the immigrants have undergone.

And why the middle class? Why should the middle class represent the new society? Because the bourgeois society, however imperfectly, embodies the norms and values of the crucial element in what the immigrants have to accommodate to.

When we speak of the "success" of an immigrant group we refer to the whole array of norms and practices they submit to: earning a living, acquiring possessions, educating their children, and instilling in them some version of freedom of ideas, opinion, and expression. Both political discussion and polite controversy—are of the essence.

It is often said that many Arab countries have had in their history no Enlightenment movement to compare to Western Europe's. That may or may not be the case. What counts is that in the here and now of Dutch society, they are offered the fruits of that movement and take them. We know that many have, and have done so eagerly. They are the middle-class Moroccans with professions, good Dutch, children at the university, and summer homes abroad. Most visibly they are writers like Hafid Bouazza, whose early story "Apolline" is still a beautiful allegory of the irresistible attractions and rewards offered by the new world of old Europe.

But what of the ones who do not take such opportunities? They may be second or third generation, the product of families in which the father has either returned to Morocco or simply lost control or become irrelevant with his old ways in this new setting. The sons—it's usually men who don't or can't—are not able or inclined to adjust to this modern European society. And since certain cultural styles have never ceased existing in these families, those styles now assert themselves with a vengeance against the new country. The result is inevitably anti-social.

I'm not speaking of those who are simply working class and respectably stay so, but of the problematic ones who are generally, though somewhat vaguely, referred to as the underclass.

Where there is a sense of alienation or exclusion, a segment of an outgroup will develop a mixture of old values and new ghetto styles and use that blend to express a hostility to the dominant culture. This will last as long as the sense of cultural disaffinity does. Such a style becomes both self-definition and weapon, creating a strange mixture of hostility and intimacy with the new country.

Inevitably, such a group will then be stigmatized by the dominant culture, as much for its style and values as its behavior and actions. The ensuing vicious cycle spells not so much a clash of cultures as a clash of styles.

These young men are the ones, unfortunately, who figure prominently in the media. Let us not forget that long before Muslim extremism became the big worry in Europe, it was immigrant crime, and in Holland especially Moroccan crime, that the native population feared. In part, this criminal behavior is nothing more than the classic juvenile delinquency of the underclass. Without necessarily being gang members, they often favor certain values, styles, speech—a mixture of Dutch, Arabic, and even African languages.

In the relationship to crime, their situation resembles that of African American young men in the US, where incarceration rates for black men are shockingly disproportionate to the general population. While their cultural situations, their backgrounds and history, might be entirely different, their positions, the role they play in the society, are similar. Obviously there is no Islam involved in the plight of African Americans and no slavery in Moroccans' background, but both groups favor styles and modes uncommon in the majority society. Obviously too, when the old style can fit into the new—African American "gangsta rap" in the US entertainment industry, for instance —the match turns out to be mutually beneficial, but this is rare, and we don't know if such a match is available in the Netherlands for its Moroccan underclass.

The Left, of course, whether in Europe or the United States, blames discrimination and holds the society responsible. The Right calls it social pathology and blames the criminal. The Right asserts that words like 'discrimination' never cover the story, and the Left holds that the dominant society never gives full credit to the victimization of the newcomers. The realistic but benevolent Middle seems to be unaware of the values and styles such groups adhere to.

What are these styles? Underclass young Moroccans have been studied extensively by, among others, the criminologist Frank van Gemert, who believes that traits which served Moroccan Berbers well in the Rif Mountain culture of scarcity and rivalry now figure in Amsterdam-West and Rotterdam-Zuid.

He singles out suspiciousness as one such trait—an almost tribal lack of trust in any outsider. You are ever vigilant, not because someone has done you wrong but because he may— so before he takes advantage, you thwart him.

This stance is not merely self-protective. It is aggressive. Young Moroccan men exhibit a perennially challenging attitude, always provoking others, never trusting them. They achieve honor by doing so, and in the process may rely on violence and cunning. Some attribute this to street culture, not Moroccan culture: violence and intimidation bring respect on urban streets everywhere.

Appearance is crucial. Certain behavioral styles come about as a safeguard against discovery. Suspiciousness is concealed so you won't give yourself away; you highlight a seeming truth—hence in comportment and speech, the desired reality is elevated over the actual.

These cultural values not only clash with the dominant norms but in effect undermine them. After all, the individualism of a more or less democratic society is made possible by a certain trust and cooperation. Doing well in a European school, or at work, requires a lessening of suspicion and a rejection of strict hierarchy, or at least the tacit consent to a somewhat disguised hierarchy. And reporting what you want instead of what is strikes Europeans as "lying."

Which is of course not to say that every young Moroccan in the Netherlands becomes a criminal. It is to say, though, that the fairly large underclass remains and will continue to remain a restive part of the population for many decades to come. While the African American underclass is generally estimated at about forty percent of the US Black population, probably the Dutch economic safety net prevents such a large percentage from existing in the Netherlands. But it is significant enough, and unassimilable enough, and sufficiently un-bourgeois, to remain, like its African American counterpart, a troubling, somewhat unintegrated, part of the larger society.

All of which leaves one question unanswered: Are these the young Moroccans who become candidates for Jihad?

Yes and no: Some few are, especially when they convert from criminal life to extreme religion, often through the intercession of a radical imam. Paradoxically, they see themselves as "going straight." But a larger number of terrorist players on the European scene—though in absolute terms still small—are those middle-class kids, whose parents have had a bit of success in the West but have not been able to guide their children out of the two worlds they inhabit. They're educated enough to have political opinions, or aversions to certain policies, or convictions about cultural superiority. They are believers and revengists and they subscribe to causes. We have as much to fear from dreamers and "idealists" as from criminals.

2008

Acculturating Muslims in the West: More Complex in Europe than America (with Youssef Azghari)

In 2007 we wrote an article, "Identity and Diversity: Muslims in the US and Europe," which was originally published in English in *The West Portal Monthly* and in Dutch in the prominent daily *NRC Handelsblad*. Since then, the piece has been reprinted many times and frequently cited, not only in numerous popular magazines and scholarly journals, but in books as well. Evidently it touched a nerve.

We compared the US to Europe in its reception of Muslim immigrants and made the following points:

America's absorption of immigrants, we thought, was easier and much quicker. In the case of its Muslim immigrants, we noted that most Muslims who came to the US were middle class, and managed for themselves to make their integration easier.

We also pointed out that immigrants into the US came of their own accord, while the first waves of Muslim immigrants into Europe were recruited as guest workers or arrived as political refugees. Those who came to America fended for themselves, while the ones who came to Europe retained a greater dependence on employers and ultimately governments.

The comparison we made that apparently hit home with many readers is that America played the role of the hard-headed father who let his grown-up kids struggle for themselves, while Europe was the softer mother ever ready to lend a helping hand. This metaphor has its roots in the historical growth of America as against that of Europe. America, comprised after all of people whose forebears had different cultural roots, was from the start used to new immigrants who came to the country of unlimited opportunities on their own to build a future.

Not so in Europe where—despite recent cooperation between various European political elites—nationalism and a sort of "our people first" sentiment still flourish, and where support for immigrants was never unqualified. In the aftermath of World War Two, they were needed as cheap labor, and it was expected that they (as well as more recent refugees) either return home or adjust to the majority culture. That culture was marked by equal treatment for men and women, no discrimination between religions or sexual preference, and respect for freedom of expression.

These worthy universal values became the sticking point for strictly brought up Fundamentalist Muslims. Apparently unlimited freedom included freedom to insult their most cherished beliefs. The attack on Charlie Hebdo in Paris was an extremist response against the perceived insult to the Prophet Muhammad. Though Westernized Muslims frequently use freedom of expression to argue for their own rights, it is the perceived abuse of that freedom that has led to the violent acts that obviously intensified the negative European image of Muslims.

With the hindsight of 2016, maybe the greatest difference we saw in our article was that American culture is less circumscribed in what it regards as American acculturation than is Europe, which has certain almost "familial" expectations of what it means to be Dutch or French or German. This looseness has stood America in good stead. Its Muslims have "integrated" in the sense that they are not particularly conspicuous as Muslims. Even in this present age of terrorism, if Ahmed and Yasmina live next door and raise reasonably well-behaved children, that is, if the family's behavior does not stand out, they are accepted, however casually, as Americans.

This is less so in Europe. The Muslim family next door remains a bit alien, a bit strange, a bit "other."

It is that which makes the frequent admonition on the part of Americans that "Europe should do more to integrate its Muslims" so true—and so annoying. America is now in the position that Europe was in some forty or fifty years ago when it was scolding and lecturing the US about its race relations. Now the roles seem reversed. It is America that doesn't grasp what's involved in their integration. As Europe did not understand American complexity then, it is America now that doesn't.

True, a small part of the Muslim population no longer feels at home in Europe, but an ever larger group, born and bred there, feels more at home in Europe than in the country of their origin. That some run afoul of the law or are recruited by Jihadis for terrorism will inevitably make more news than that some run a thriving business or climb the ranks of the academy. More and more Muslims do better in the workplace, and levels of education, compared to their parents and grandparents, are rising, as inevitably more of them have entered the middle class. Such good news is not part of European awareness, but more important is that it remains culturally much harder for a European to view the Muslim family next door as fully European. Their religion is odd. Their ceremonies are different. Their embracing of local ways uncertain. Are they members of the family?

As for their opinions—about gays, or women, or human rights—Muslims are often perceived as not fully, wholeheartedly subscribing to these.

But those are political opinions. Don't we have a right to differ on those? Yes and no. These political opinions are intermixed with a set of values, which are considered crucial, essential European values.

So "integration" faces an obstacle from each side. Europeans distrust the commitment—the genuineness of the commitment—of Muslims to the European way of life. And Muslims fear a perceived European lack of standards and morals. Muslims may well see liberty as important but not as much as the values that were left behind: family, honor, obedience.

This matter of values has yet another dimension. Muslims in Europe frequently see no clear European values but a sort of vacuum, a "laissez-faire" way of living that strikes many Muslims as a moral chaos of total permissiveness, immoral or at best amoral. The European majority culture has done a poor job of convincing those newcomers that there is anything of moral substance in the European way of life at all. Our readers will ask, *Are you speaking of the majority of Muslims?* No, of course not. Most Muslims try earnestly to integrate, some of them following the role model of high-achieving Muslims in the new culture, often merging qualities from both cultures. But a big gap remains. Integration remains difficult to achieve in daily life. Combining the best of two cultures sounds simple but isn't. It requires more endurance, patience and wisdom than you'd need even to submerge yourself wholly in the new culture, which after all is what assimilation is. Ideally, the best integration would be of those who regard their background critically but also examine openly Western norms and values outside of their comfort zone.

All this is hard. Ever since the doctrine of liberty swept over the West, outsiders have pondered it, trying to understand and in some cases to practice it. Diverse as all people, including Muslims, are, they've done so with more or less success. On the whole, the cultural understanding of liberty has been a barrier. So far, it has been more difficult in Europe than in America for Muslims to be fully accepted or to accept—to be integrated or to integrate.

2016

Elusive Affinities: New Cultures in Europe

Once again, this column in my series on Muslims in Europe tries to explain the key difficulty Europe faces in integrating its recent and not so recent Muslim arrivals. Earlier waves of immigration had pretty much followed a pattern we in the US are familiar with: new immigrants struggle, but their assimilation isn't finally concluded until the second and third generation.

While this is still largely the model that obtains, a sizable minority of Muslim immigrants do not follow it. Often the second and third generation has more trouble becoming happily Europeanized than the first.

They may speak the local language, and be familiar with the ways of the only country they know, but their discomfort in Europe is real. Through a mixture of personal resentment and outside religious propaganda, a small but significant segment turns to crime, or is susceptible to being radicalized.

Dutch-born Moroccan young men (always men, not women) are vastly over-represented in the criminal justice system of the Netherlands. French-born Algerian young men are disproportionately radicalized. Young

Turkish-Germans form an ever more unstable element in German society. I could go on.

How to explain it?

My view is that assimilation is always hardest when the culture of origin differs radically from the culture of the new society. Arab cultures of the Middle East and North Africa revolve around a kind of Islam-induced authoritarianism, an absolutist impulse, which the new country sets itself against. Certain standards—deference to parents, obedience to government, respect for force—are in those parts of the world accepted almost without question, while European cultures encourage their citizens to question them.

The newcomer, especially if he's young, mistakes this seeming laxness for total permissiveness, an absence of all standards, and is almost surprised when the host culture clamps down and jails him for a criminal offense. European culture seems amorphous, without clear values and beliefs. Freedom looks like the absence of morality. Since so few absolute standards obtain, why shouldn't you grope and fondle women at a public celebration—especially when they're so provocatively dressed?

This disaffinity between the two cultures makes assimilation extraordinarily difficult, especially since assimilation entails accepting the morals, the norms, the mores, of the new culture. Genuine multiculturalism is an abstraction; one culture has to dominate.

Lately, some of the young Arabs in Europe have been saying, "Why shouldn't *we* dominate? Our culture is better, our religion superior—therefore our time has come!" That is essentially the view of "Sharia 4 Belgium." The idea of such notions gliding smoothly into modern Western society is absurd. No such fit is possible.

The disaffinity of the two cultures creates a virtual incompatibility. And, in fact, it's not as if the world hasn't seen it before: surely there was a cultural component to the slaughter of American Indians. Whatever the differences between the tribes, say, the mild Hopis and the warlike Apaches, could Western European settlers have lived happily next to either one or co-existed comfortably with a thriving Indian culture? Only nostalgia or sentimentality—or retrospective guilt—of the victors, the conquerors, could think so, or make it appear so in fantasy or films.

What, then, will happen in Europe? One likely outcome is that somehow, in ways we can't quite foresee now, one culture will emerge the winner, at tragic cost to the other.

2016

Two Cultures, Two Attitudes

C ultural critics in the nineteenth century were quicker to make generalizations about culture than we are, or perhaps less careful.

In earlier times, Heinrich Heine, the German poet and critic, and Matthew Arnold, the English Victorian man of letters, spoke of two strands of thought, those of "Hebraism" and "Hellenism." Biblical Jews emphasized behavior and morality, while the ancient Greeks were lighter, more inclined to let the mind roam free.

I often think of that distinction when the discussion turns to assimilating Muslims into Western European cultures.

A marvelous scene in the 2006 French film "Days of Glory" ("*Indigènes*"), about colonial North African Arab volunteers in the French Army during World War Two, shows an evening of ballet to be enjoyed by the troops. French and Arabs alike are at the performance, but one after another, the Arabs slip out. The scene is probably puzzling to anyone unaware of the cultural differences between European and Arab cultures. To the Arabs, the ballet is an unseemly display of female flesh and a foolish, inappropriate exhibition of acrobatics.

Some have called this tendency in Arab cultures puritanical, but that word is at best a kind of crude shorthand. It is not a rejection of the flesh as much as a dislike of impropriety and frivolity. But the lightness and elegance of art is the very thing that Western culture has favored. Art was a way to banish gloom and sometimes encapsulate the culture's highest aspirations.

Muslims have their own art, of course, but they do not regard it as being akin to their highest cultural values. Where Western art became ever more an embodiment of the best in its culture and a rival to religion and morality, art in Muslim countries did not replace religion, or values like the patriarchy, the loyalty to family, and the obedience of young people. Anything that rivals God or morality would be perceived as a rebellion against Islam. The "puritanism" of the Arabs is the fear that fanatically pursued pleasure, whether in art or sex, could rival the love of God and thereby lessen adherence to Prophet and Faith.

So for most Muslims the pleasures of aestheticism, except when they serve the religion as in a splendid mosque, remain a lesser pleasure, whereas in the post-Enlightenment West it has often been worshiped ardently, especially in societies that have proclaimed "the death of God." Certainly Muslims could never subscribe to what happened in the West in the nineteenth century when art virtually took the place of God, nor could Muslim societies endorse values only derived from art. Art as a value, a belief, a guide, had little relevance to them. In this, they're not all that different from Western society in the time of the religious wars.

The unlikeness of the two cultures in this regard is one more disaffinity that may stand in the way of easy assimilation. At the very least, it requires Muslims to accept the Western view of art. "Cultural hybridity" seems to me to exist only on paper. There have, of course, been art-loving westernized Muslim in Europe who have jumped over and braved stern disapproval of parents, family, tribe. But for most it remains one of many obstacles.

2017

Afterword

Muslims in Europe: Notes, Comments, Questions

1)   **A**t a San Francisco gathering many years ago—seven or eight of us around an elegant table—the dinner party conversation turned to the endless war in Afghanistan. One guest mused aloud that she so wished some of those Afghani men, whether Taliban or not, could be brought to Marin County for a few weeks. "I think it would really open their eyes."

Yes, it's funny, of course, but there's a sweetness to it, an American generosity and innocence. Be kind, be warm, be hospitable—Show Them Our Way of Life, and They'll See The Light.

The likelihood is that those men would return home and fanatically reaffirm their own culture. You can just hear them afterwards saying to their friends. "Those weak American men let their women run around free with practically nothing on."

I don't think European naïveté equals American naïveté, but Europeans too can be self-deluded. Their equivalent is to say, "Our laws, our freedoms, our safety—once fully understood—will triumph."

Will they?

2) All matters of assimilation, integration, the yielding of one culture to another, are poorly understood, and on the whole not easily talked about. Discussing cultural difference sounds intolerant, and certainly judging another culture feels taboo. The underlying sentiment remains that cultures should be judged on their own terms. Nor do generalizations about culture ever seem to make much sense. What does it really mean for one culture to value "hospitality," given the number of different things we mean by that word and the way we can be "hospitable" about some things and not others?

3) I have heard Arabists speak about the Honor and Shame cultures of the Middle East and North Africa, in contrast to the Guilt and Responsibility culture of the West, but I've also heard these things about Scotch-Irish Honor and Shame culture, and Southern US culture, and Prison culture, and Gang culture. Certainly if you "disrespect" someone in any of the latter, you will be treated harshly. But how close to one another are those cultures? Not close at all. So how meaningful is this observation?

4) In discussions of this subject people turn with palpable relief from culture to politics, which latter is easier to fathom. Yet politics derives from culture, and to look at political qualities as more persuasive than cultural is to misunderstand the emotional appeal of a culture. Would

a solid system of rights and laws persuade someone to give his or her heart to that culture? Does getting rights create more warmth?

5) Political answers too are favored in explanations of motives. But people explain themselves by often self-servingly interpreting their own maladjustment as a form of righteous anger. The human lust for self-justification and indignation is embraced almost sensually. It's not, as some have argued, Western politically correct explanations that have supplied non-assimilating Muslims their reasons and rationalizations—rather, the latter's nameless, disorienting anger may have searched for a cause to explain and justify itself.

How reliable are our own explanations of our behavior?

2017

Printed in the United States
By Bookmasters